the elusive celt

Perceptions of Traditional Irish Music Communities in Europe

Rina Schiller

Ⴔ Carysfort Press

Peter Lang

Oxford · Bern · Berlin · Bruxelles · New York · Wien

Bibliographic information published by Die Deutsche Nationalbibliothek.
Die Deutsche Nationalbibliothek lists this publication in the Deutsche
Nationalbibliografie; detailed bibliographic data is available on the Internet at
http://dnb.d-nb.de.

A catalogue record for this book is available from the British Library.

Library of Congress Cataloging-in-Publication Data

Names: Schiller, Rina, author.
Title: The elusive Celt : perceptions of traditional Irish music
    communities in Europe / Rina Schiller.
Description: Oxford ; New York : Peter Lang, 2022. | Includes
    bibliographical references and index.
Identifiers: LCCN 2021032572 (print) | LCCN 2021032573 (ebook) | ISBN
    9781800795723 (paperback) | ISBN 9781800795730 (ebook) | ISBN
    9781800795747 (epub)
Subjects: LCSH: Celtic music--Europe--History and criticism. | Folk
    music--Europe--History and criticism. | Folk music--Ireland--History and
    criticism.
Classification: LCC ML3580 .S35 2022 (print) | LCC ML3580 (ebook) | DDC
    781.62/91604--dc21
LC record available at https://lccn.loc.gov/2021032572
LC ebook record available at https://lccn.loc.gov/2021032573

Cover image: Music travelling from Ireland to continental Europe
Cover design by Brian Melville for Peter Lang.

ISBN   978-1-80079-572-3 (print)
ISBN   978-1-80079-573-0 (ePDF)
ISBN   978-1-80079-574-7 (ePub)

© Peter Lang Group AG 2022

Published by Peter Lang Ltd, International Academic Publishers,
52 St Giles, Oxford, OX1 3LU, United Kingdom
oxford@peterlang.com, www.peterlang.com

This publication has been peer reviewed.

To all the musicians who have shared their music with me
Bíodh rath ar bhur gceol

Contents

Plates and Illustrations

Acknowledgements

Many people have contributed at different stages to this project that has been taking shape over the last two decades, and my sincere gratitude goes to them all. First and foremost, I would like to thank all the musicians without whose generous help its completion would indeed have been impossible. They have kept me updated about little changes that had taken place in their local Irish music communities when I revisited their sessions at annual or biannual intervals, encouraging me that my ethnographic notes will eventually materialise onto the printed page. Special thanks go to Václav Bernard and the teachers at Bernard's Summer School in Prague for allowing me access to their classes.

Many thanks are also due to all readers who have commented on successive drafts of the manuscript, in particular to Méabh Ní Fhuartháin for highlighting an aspect of non-verbal communications at Irish sessions in the chapter about authenticities that needed to be discussed in more detail, to Mary Louise O'Donnell for her excellent detailed reading suggestions, to David O'Kane for reading parts of the draft while holidaying in Berlin (and for his spontaneous contribution to the Irish session at the Blarney Pub), to Martin Stokes for moral support at a crucial phase of the project and for his observant and thoughtful comments what to consider for the final draft, and to the anonymous reader for highlighting the desirability of making discussions of academic issues as accessible as possible to non-academic readers.

Further, I would like to thank the group *Bal Feirste* and Maryvonne Le Roy for sharing their Breton repertoire with me, David Le Bourhis for the loan of his collection of *Tri Yann* CDs, Petra Honkysova for help with Czech translations, and the Snapper for a lucky snap. I am also most grateful to Dusty for his patient assistance to numerous little hiccups for which my computer needed attention from time to time, to Sandy Cheyne for permission to reproduce samples of his drawings of Berlin musicians, and to David Bird for providing an essential single note for the manuscript.

A special thanks goes to staff at the McClay Library of Queen's University Belfast for trying their best to make reading material available under the most difficult conditions of Covid-19 restrictions. And last but not least I would like to express my delight and thanks to staff at Carysfort/ Peter Lang Publishers for their supportive, flexible, and accommodating ways to take the manuscript through to its printed form.
Many thanks to you all.

Rina Schiller, July 2021

Plate 1. The former *Irish Club*, a small B&B with bar facilities in the north of Prague

Plate 2. Dave Bradfield's *Tír na nÓg* Celtic craft and music shop in Berlin

Plate 3. Performance at the end of Bernard's Summer School at Prague's Ponec Theatre

Plate 4. *Taksim Square* with the *Taksim Anıtı* – the Monument of the Republic in Istanbul

Plate 5. *Taksim Square* in Istanbul during the *Gezi Park* protests in 2013

Introduction

'So what aspect of traditional Irish music is your research project about?', asked my friend Jamie as he was dandering down the garden path with the banjo slung over his shoulder. We were on our way to the local session, passing the time with a little light conversation. During its troubled recent past Irish traditional musicians in Belfast got used to walk in groups to session venues because some Loyalists in Northern Irish society like to ascribe political associations to the genre – as indeed to everything 'Irish' – and musicians carrying instruments are known to have been attacked on their way to sessions. Nationalist ideologies in the North of Ireland can also lead to aggressive behaviour towards musicians, as I describe in Chapter 1 in the discussion of the mixed fortunes of the guitar in Irish traditional music. The area in which I live is fairly mixed in all regards, but there you have it: traditional musicians in Belfast have learned to be careful.

So here we were on our way to the local session, having a little chat about music, and Jamie's mate Breandan immediately interjected, 'Irish music doesn't need studied, it develops very well on its own.' Anne hid behind her fiddle case and pretended not to hear what we were talking about. Fintan, beside her, also kept himself out of the conversation. He is known for his opinion that 'mixed blood' prevents musicians from playing Irish traditional music 'properly'. It is not entirely clear though, what exactly is supposed to constitute 'mixed blood'. In politically charged contexts of Belfast it may or may not indicate very specific meanings of imagined ethnicities. I was already feeling regret for having mentioned the topic at all. People with an academic background in music seem to get a very poor reputation nowadays, at least within certain contexts in my home town of Belfast.

Fortunately Irish traditional musicians at European locations, with whose music-making this book is concerned, were not quite so hostile to the study of music, and they didn't have any concerns about 'mixed blood' either. Indeed musicians from widely different backgrounds came together to play this genre within the contexts that I describe in this book. Many of them have been involved in playing this music for many years, and an inquiry into their music-making activities is a novel approach to the topic of Irish traditional music that has long been overdue.

The study of Irish traditional music has a chequered history. Before the 1970s it was only maverick individuals like Richard Henebry (1928) or Francis O'Neill (1903, 1913) who paid detailed attention to the genre. Within the field of ethnomusicology Irish traditional music started only in the 1980s to 1990s to gain serious attention, and studies of the genre and its social contexts outside Ireland have focused largely on the English-speaking traditional destinations of Irish emigration: England, America, and Australia (Moloney 1992, Uí Ógáin 1996, Williams 1996, Smith 1997). The same can be observed in non-musical studies concerned with influences of changing political developments on image and identity constructions in diasporic Irish communities. An illustrative recent example is Brian M. Walker's (2019) study of oral history constructions within Irish diasporic communities.

The possibility of an instrumental musical genre transferring well to non-English-speaking contexts seems to have been mostly circumvented in studies of Irish music and culture. Where the international interest of musicians in the genre was mentioned, it tended to have been portrayed as insignificant (cf. Wilkinson 2002), often surrounded with an aura of suspicion as regards musical 'authenticity'. Occasionally, voices could even be heard that emigrant musicians were 'losing their authenticity' and that 'the pure drop' could only be found in Ireland (cf. Tansey 1996). Such ethnically motivated nationalism can make unprejudiced perceptions of music-making difficult. A brave thrust into new explorations was Desi Wilkinson's study of the label 'Celtic' in the traditional music scene of Brittany and other 'Celtic genres' (Wilkinson 1999, 2003), and Malcolm Chapman's studies of the label of 'Celtic music' (Chapman 1992, 1994) have shown that this is a rather flexible category indeed, as far as its contents are concerned. For my own research the question then presented itself how 'the Celtic' was imagined by musicians elsewhere in Europe.

Fortunately, in the 1990s Martin Stokes was still teaching ethnomusic-ology at Queen's University Belfast. He was a major influence on my aca-demic thought development, and he encouraged my further thinking along the lines of traditional Irish musicians within different cultural contexts being just as 'authentic' to their own cultural environments as those within the home context of Ireland. This gave rise to my developing an interest in how different aspects associated with traditional Irish music may or may not well transfer to different cultural contexts, and what the respective reasons for this might be. In essence, it is another posing of the question of how ethnocentrism may colour our perceptions of what people at dif-ferent locations are doing with a particular genre of music, in this case traditional Irish music. The fine-tuning of the main research focus for the developing project became then: do European musicians construct their own 'authenticities' in relation to playing traditional Irish music sessions within their own communities or do concepts of 'authenticity' travel with the genre, and how do they see their music-making in relation to Ireland, to Europe, to 'the Celtic', and to their native musical traditions? This focus was best served by using descriptions, rather than transcriptions, to convey musical activities at the investigated community contexts, thereby ad-dressing a general readership as well as musical specialists and a variety of academic interest areas.

My field research access was made easy by a lifelong background of having played music, as a child with my mother who played an eclectic repertoire on the mandolin, as a singer and guitarist touring the European continent in the 1970s with Irish and non-Irish musicians, and since the early 1980s, when I moved to Belfast, as a participant in numerous trad-itional community sessions where I played mandolin, whistle, concertina, and bodhrán. From this musical background I had a solid grounding in skills to participate during my research in session playing on various levels of proficiency, which facilitated communication with the respective local Irish music communities.

Methodologically I have resorted to a variety of tools: informal interviewing, participant observation, questionnaires, and analysis of visual images associated with music merchandise and with media representations. Frequently also information was offered to me voluntarily, of which the research community thought that it might be of interest for my project. At various times over the years I have rechecked with musicians for feedback on drafts for this project, hoping thereby to avoid misrepresentations. As the project has a rather wide scope, this was of course not possible with everyone who participated in all the surveyed Irish music-making contexts, but I hope that the overall descriptions will meet everyone's agreement. Field research at the discussed locations was carried out in Berlin from 2004 annually or biannually during Belfast university holiday times, in Prague and Vienna from 2007, in the Balkan area in 2007 and 2012, and in Istanbul annually from 2012 to 2019, at which time travel and field research became impossible because of the outbreak of the Covid-19 pandemic. Even if travel had been possible, no community sessions were taking place anywhere. The continuation of my research had become impossible by worldwide environmental circumstances.

What has fascinated me about traditional Irish music from the beginning is that it is a migratory genre. Let me explain this a little further. All music travels. People pick up a piece of music here, take it there, and pass it on to someone else who continues this process. In the age of the Internet this process can speed up considerably. But in the twentieth century, for traditional Irish music some very specific process has taken place, turning it into a migratory genre. That is, the music travels to different cultural contexts with a set of extra-musical expectations attached to it, which people observe when playing this music within their own informal community contexts.

Cynics might argue that it is Irish pub culture that has been exported internationally in the twentieth century. But not all pubs have Irish music sessions, and not all sessions take place in pubs. To understand the music and its processes, it was clear from the beginning that I would have to focus considerably closer on the music itself and let go of a lot of the old clichés. In his seminal publication *Ethnicity, Identity and Music* Stokes (1994:97–115) has described in detail how music travels to different contexts and how meanings of music are created, negotiated, adapted, and changed, in particular when leaving their 'home context'. Stokes shows convincingly how detailed ethnographic descriptions are an essential means to make sense of what takes place at cross-cultural community music-making encounters; so attention to ethnographic detail was an essential tool for my research.

And here we already meet an essential distinguishing mark of traditional Irish music at the present point in time (the early twenty-first century). In the age of the Internet many musical genres travel easily, but since the 1970s time of the European folk revival, traditional Irish music has continually grown in international attention. This applies not only on the commercial level of often showy stage performances, but also to community music aspects of this genre, as they are performed by groups of traditional Irish music enthusiasts who meet at community venues at regular intervals to perform this music informally at locally organised 'traditional sessions'.

Most helpful was my good fortune of learning during my undergraduate days from Martin Stokes how to play Turkish folk music on the bağlama, the long-necked lute commonly used in playing Turkish folk music. This increased my sensitivity for observing possible commonalities between Irish and Turkish folk music, and this theme also emerged as a possible link during my research with Irish music in Berlin, where I found a significantly large Turkish population in many locations where I was working, with some possible connections suggesting themselves between the two cultures. As it turned out, such stylistic similarities were more easily admitted by Turkish-Irish musicians in Istanbul than by Berlin Irish musicians. Within Irish home session contexts, however, I found such awareness of stylistic similarities strikingly absent.

In his historical look at traditional music in Irish society, Martin Dowling has carried out interviews with contemporary Belfast community musicians, who refer to a certain 'punchiness' of a 'Belfast style' as a result of the banjo having been a very popular instrument for traditional sessions in the 1970s to early 1980s in Belfast (Dowling 2014:308–10). I do not doubt that 'esteem of social groupings' will have influenced the development of Belfast traditional playing styles. It is, however, difficult to decide whether popularity of banjo playing has led to a certain 'punchiness' especially in Belfast flute playing, or whether an emerging 'punchiness' in Belfast playing styles has suggested to musicians a connection with the previous popularity of the banjo in Belfast traditional sessions.

Most detailed as Dowling's historical research may have been, it is nevertheless bound to be selective just as much as any other approach will be. Even the 'punchiness' of a playing style is to a certain extent influenced by image constructions of social groupings, and its meaning will certainly change depending on the respective circumstances. For the broad scope of my research project an historical approach would indeed have been impossible and would at best have led to meandering through the ages and guessing from archaeological objects the possible influences or non-influences of migrating Celtic peoples. As my interest was more on how and why musicians construct perceived links with these ancient cultures in their contemporary music-making, I have decided to limit myself to ethnographic descriptions of present-day European community contexts of Irish session playing.

The question that presents itself immediately when deciding on a multi-sited ethnography is to delineate on which aspects to focus and what to leave out of the discussion as not relevant to the central topic of the study. It was therefore unavoidable that I had to limit my scope of investigations, resulting in my choice of image constructions about Ireland and 'the Celtic', and how which Irish session concepts transfer with the musical genre to the investigated different European locations.

In his analysis and deconstruction of present elusive images of 'the Celtic' Simon James (1999:19) mentions that in recent years the image of the Celts has been interpreted as a 'pan-European prehistoric fore-runner of the European Union', and that 'such was the message of the major exhibition *I Celti* held in Venice in 1991'. Since the concept of 'Celtic regions' is at present strongly linked with performances of traditional Irish music, an investigation of the elusive images of 'the Celt' presented itself as essential for understanding how musicians of this genre in Ireland and in continental Europe perceive each other in relation to their local session events. On occasion musical identifications were quite difficult to disentangle because in Ireland 'our music' is understood to refer to Irish music while in European contexts 'our music' often can refer to European music – which by geographical definition would include Irish music.

The main linking strand for deciding on the locations for my comparative European project emerged during my initial fieldwork in Berlin, where my attention was drawn to the issue of changing borders and influences of recent histories. The physical borders between recent state-socialist and free-market economy countries termed the 'Iron Curtain' had disappeared at the time of my research. But as Rüdiger Görner (2013:52) has pointed out: 'Borders redefine themselves in our consciousness and collective memory. This is why borders of the past are often more present in us than the borders of today.'

It is therefore not surprising that I found influences of the former Iron Curtain on past and present perceptions of Irish culture, and as a consequence on present-day community music-making of traditional Irish music. Images are constructed inside the mind of individual people, but they are shaped and transformed by multiple outside influences, including collective perceptions. As I found out during my inquiries, images of Irish music and Irish culture do not easily cross past political borderlines. It is here that I have located the main focus of my research, which during the last two decades has taken me to a number of locations on both sides of the former Iron Curtain, from the Baltic to the Bosphorus.

Despite discussions of past influences the comparative nature of my project required a synchronic rather than a diachronic approach by nesting questions of historical development into the discussion of their present-day effects. For instance, notions of what is 'traditional' or not are certainly not irrelevant for musicians who play music of a 'traditional genre'. The categories may at a closer look not have a long history at all; they may be arbitrary, flexible, or shifting, but they will definitely not be irrelevant. Investigations of concepts of 'traditional' and 'authentic' were components of my field of enquiry, and in Chapter 2 I try to untangle what different authenticities were of primary relevance to my study.

And then there was this interesting question of what is constructed as being a 'Celtic' cultural region or not at the present point in time. Historical evidence indicates that Celtic tribes were given to quite a lot of migration during the last few millennia, and that their cultural influences extended considerably wider than over the present region of Europe. Therefore 'Celtic links' could have been constructed more or less at all the locations where I carried out research about present-day performances of traditional Irish music. As it turned out, in some contexts such links had high relevance, in some contexts a little, and in some none at all.

Malcolm Chapman (1992, 1994) has pointed out how some countries have recently become 'thoroughly Celtic', while those that are regarded as the original 'Celtic homelands' are presently not regarded as Celtic at all. The elusive 'Celtic' connection is therefore observably arbitrary. For instance, Fintan Vallely's *Companion to Irish Traditional Music* (1999) mentions neither France, Germany, Austria, nor the Czech Republic as relevant for 'Celtic' and for 'traditional Irish music', but it discusses in detail Brittany and – interestingly – Finland as relevant for this connection. The original sites of the Celtic *La Tène* and *Hallstatt* cultures, on the other hand, are not even faintly considered as having Celtic connections. So it would seem that even in a reference work on traditional Irish music we are guided by arbitrary perspectives of the respective authors. This is not surprising, as the present concept of 'the Celtic' is an extremely flexible cultural construct, open to diverse interpretations that rarely relate to archaeological evidence or geography, and definitely not to questions of ethnicity.

Simon James (1999) has offered an interesting approach how to disentangle the reasons how and why the image of Celticity as a cultural Other has provided us with an elusive Celt by conflating Celtic languages and 'Celtic people'. As it turned out these images made their appearance in relation to conceptualisations and merchandise of Irish/Celtic music within Irish as well as continental European contexts. Certainly an historical approach could have investigated the possibilities of actual cultural influences, even if depending on projection, but since the cultural is as much constructed as the social (cf. Berger & Luckmann 1967), my research interests were rather focused on *how* cultural roots connections are constructed at different European locations *at this present point in time*. This is an interesting question, as musical styles are much open to interpretation, especially for instrumental genres. In his MA thesis (1991:10–11) Desi Wilkinson argues that by community agreement a 'Belfast style' for playing traditional Irish music can exist even if it is not actually identifiable by listening. His argument is in close agreement with Stokes' (1994) interpretation of community music-making as Wilkinson observes that 'to construct a "style" has a lot to do with the esteem of a social grouping, from within and without and their existence in time and space'.

A most important aspect for transferring musical styles, repertoires, and indeed extra-musical information is the availability of access. In this regard the Wall between eastern and western Europe in the twentieth century was indeed quite solid. Irish records, tapes, or printed music were – with very few exceptions – not obtainable on the eastern side, and the same applied to Irish-made musical instruments and related paraphernalia. In the case studies of Chapter 5 I illustrate how material culture certainly also has an influence on musical styles. Undoubtedly musical information is also transmitted through live performances, and some touring musicians occasionally were permitted to visit eastern European countries. However, communications were also restricted through language problems, since access to the English language was extremely limited in countries on the eastern side of this cultural-political fault line.

State control was prevalent in many areas of everyday life. For instance, in the 1980s in the GDR even informal get-togethers of musicians in local pubs for playing Irish music were not permitted. This led to such absurd situations as when an Irish-born musician living in West Berlin and a German-born musician living in East Berlin had to travel to Prague for occasional get-togethers to play traditional Irish music with each other.

Prague is indeed a special place in this regard for, although official culture in the twenty-first century is still attached in many areas to eastern political values, musicians find niches for playing high quality pub sessions of traditional Irish music in totally out-of-the-way locations. The official 'Irish Pubs' in the city centre, on the other hand, feature mostly a 'tourist-friendly' mixture of Anglo-American popular music, with bits of Irish music strewn into the repertoire at intervals every now and then. There are reasons for this set-up: they relate to concepts of 'session etiquette', which are discussed in detail in Chapter 4.

Crossing over the nowadays mostly invisible east/west dividing line for having a look at the Irish music scene in Vienna, I encountered a wide variety of venues with regular traditional music sessions featuring comparable repertoires to Irish home sessions, at which Irish, Scottish, and local musicians participated. Most of these sessions took place in cultural venues such as cafés or bookshops rather than in pubs, and many of the musicians attending the sessions had many years' experience of playing this musical genre. It was obvious that I was finding myself again on the western side of the former Iron Curtain. All sessions in Vienna were open to newcomers, whether they took place in pubs or in other venues, and interestingly neither musicians in Vienna, nor their colleagues in Prague, showed any interest in possible 'Celtic connections' of their geographical location within the ancient 'Celtic heartlands'.

For my comparative study I have tried to listen to as many voices as possible, so as to obtain different viewpoints, and I have tried to reflect how they relate to each other and to their wider socio-cultural environment. The study will of necessity be incomplete, as it is impossible to include *all* locations on either side of the twentieth-century European political fault line, but such 'completeness' would not be necessary anyway, since my intention was merely to show major cultural strands that are common to present-day community performances of traditional Irish music at various – and quite different – European locations (and indeed beyond).

The study focuses on community sessions of Irish traditional music as grassroots events that have a very specific performance structure. As such they are indeed not 'performances' in the sense of being provided for an audience, but communicative events between musicians of this genre that offer space for exchanging related social information, and they follow specific guidelines that I explain in Chapter 4. It is certainly most interesting that these extra-musical guidelines to social etiquette have transferred to all these Irish traditional music contexts in Europe that I describe in my study.

Conceptual Organisation

The study follows an imaginary trail through community contexts of traditional Irish music-making, where the image of the 'elusive Celt' may be invoked in a multiplicity of ways. It is not a study of possible distributions of genetic ethnicities, but rather of how their relevance can be socially constructed to ascribe labels of 'self' and 'other' within musical contexts.

Chapter 1 introduces the musical genre, its stylistic specifics, and which instruments are nowadays most commonly used in its community performance contexts. Ascriptions of suitability and 'traditionality' have changed over time, as have those of relative status of individual instruments, and in the organological section I set these in relation to how they have been discussed by different writers in the associated literature. Ascriptions are social constructs, malleable and context-dependent, and therefore no definitive one-fits-all description can be given. The listed examples of repertoires provide a representative overview of investigated performance contexts. They are not an in-depth description of individual repertoires and playing styles because these hold no relevance for the central topic of this study, which focuses on image constructions in relation to this musical genre.

Chapter 2 dissects the elusive concept of 'authenticity' by paying attention to the multiplicity of aspects to which it can be ascribed. To disentangle all these different 'authenticities' the chapter looks at how the subject has been approached in the related literature and then draws out conclusions to what extent these findings are applicable to community performance contexts of traditional Irish music and what aspects of 'authenticity' proved most relevant during my research.

In Chapter 3 I set the virtual sat-nav from the Baltic to the Bosphorus to identify the research locations that I have selected for my study. Multi-sited ethnographies present some problems in that the researcher has to limit the scope by fine-tuning to the specific focus of the study but extending it wide enough to make it representative. In this case the focus was on influences of recent history in Europe on image constructions of the 'elusive Celt' in relation to traditional Irish music community contexts on both sides of the former Iron Curtain. In the context of Berlin this former political dividing line ran right through the city in the form of the Berlin Wall. The other selected locations of Prague, Budapest, Vienna, and Bucharest followed the course of the former Iron Curtain, to end at the eastern edges of Europe in Istanbul, where a traditional Irish music session has been running over the last two decades. Istanbul also presented a particularly interesting location because it is located at the isthmus between geographical Europe and Asia.

Chapter 4 introduces the ethnographic intricacies that make the Irish traditional music community session different from any other musical performance contexts, suggesting that these have contributed to its rising international popularity by addressing some basic communal human needs in contemporary European society. This chapter raises questions about what extra-musical concepts are attached to these specific community performances, as well as why and how they are transmitted with the music to international contexts.

In Chapter 5 we home in on specific Irish traditional music sessions at the six countries selected for this study. We follow what musicians do within their given environment to enable performances of Irish music sessions that follow the same socio-musical arrangements as in the home contexts of Ireland. We discover that many traditional Irish session musicians dedicate considerable time, money, and effort to learn fine detail of this musical genre, a fact that is frequently drowned in superficial media reproductions of national stereotypes. This image does not always agree with perceptions of their local audiences who – influenced by media images – may interpret the 'elusive Celt' for their own purposes. However, contested images arose only in relation to non-acceptance of the specifics of the Irish session performance, which came to the fore in misconceptions of some publicans. Where these discrepancies could not be solved the musicians chose to move on to other venues. For the purpose of gaining an insight into how these local community musicians choose to interpret the image of the 'elusive Celt' for their music-making we complete the picture with an analysis of CD covers that local groups have produced of their own music.

Chapter 6 focuses the analytic eye on what qualities have been ascribed over time to the 'elusive Celt' and how they manifest nowadays within performance contexts of traditional Irish music, in Ireland and internationally. We find out about a multiplicity of meanings that have been ascribed to the 'elusive Celt', some of them with positive consequences such as artistic inspirations, others with not so positive influences such as animosities arising from ethnic nationalism. We discover that it is exactly the elusiveness and flexibility of the image that makes it so powerful because its meaning can be interpreted, negotiated, adjusted, and changed in multiple ways. The consequence of these malleable characteristics means that it can be appropriated by different groups in society for different purposes, and this may indeed be happening in some regions of Europe in relation to traditional

Irish music by interpreting the ancient Celts as a prehistoric forerunner of the European Union. Chapter 6 closes with a reflection on how the 'Celtic' was socially constructed in 1970s Brittany, where it has hugely contributed to a revival of regional folk music traditions.

It remains to be seen what community musicians in Ireland and elsewhere will make of the 'elusive Celt'. Certainly we can assert that the findings of this study testify to the combination of flexibility and robustness in the performance form of the present traditional Irish session. It remains to be hoped that we all will be able to transform the image of the 'elusive Celt' into one that will benefit us all for the future of traditional Irish music-making.

CHAPTER I

Genre, Style, and Instruments

The term 'traditional Irish music' as it is used nowadays is a multi-purpose term that can refer to a conglomeration of musical genres of a certain vintage, and the contents of this rather broad category have indeed been subject to competing definitions and negotiations. But the term may also be used in a narrow sense as referring to the genre of traditional Irish dance music, which originates mostly from the late eighteenth and early nineteenth centuries and is unified by stylistic performance aspects. All parties – musicians, theorists, and institutions – agree that this instrumental dance music is located at the core of 'traditional Irish music'.

It is this music that has found much attention of international community musicians in many different countries since the 1960s. It consists of a limited number of different dance types that are explained in detail in this chapter. However, since performers do not pick their repertoires by what fits neatly into specified musical categories, abstract classification systems are only to a certain limit useful. For instance, frequently older Irish melodies are integrated into performances, which do not belong to the body of dance music, such as compositions by the seventeenth-century harper Turlough O'Carolan (1670–1738), which enjoy much popularity at sessions. These are in session contexts stylistically aligned to those of the dance music tradition. This point applies to Irish as well as to other contexts. Musicians perceive the contents of these performances as a unified body of music, as 'a genre' in the sense of something being perceived as different from, say, Rembetika, or Jazz. It is this broader meaning I have in mind when I speak here of 'this genre of music'.

Irish Music and Dance

Over the last few centuries a number of dance types have come to Ireland from various European countries, partly via England. The late eighteenth- and early nineteenth-century Irish Dancing Masters, for instance, were strongly influenced by French culture (cf. Murphy 1995, Brennan 1999). Elements of the related European musical traditions were absorbed into the Irish tradition, where they developed their particular Irish stylistic characteristics. These common cultural roots seem to hold little relevance today, whereas common 'Celtic' roots of what is presently regarded as 'Celtic' have come to hold significant relevance in some contexts, and this contemporary system of classification also influences presentations of the music in academic texts. For instance, Fintan Vallely's *Companion to Irish Traditional Music* (1999) does not mention France, Austria or Germany as relevant for traditional Irish music, but it discusses in detail Brittany (two and a half pages) and – surprisingly – Finland (two pages). Brittany is of course nowadays considered a 'Celtic' country, and some Breton dances are frequently included where modern Irish folk dancing takes place, but so far the same concept had not been applied to Finland, so its inclusion seems somewhat puzzling. This is Helen Brennan's description of the Irish dance tradition:

> … Irish society has been part of the wider European cultural scene for many cen- turies, and all of our group dances have international connections. The modern Irish dance formations derive from both the European mediaeval long-line and couple dances and incorporate elements of both forms. The square dances such as the group jigs and reels, the cotillon and the later quadrilles are related to the old long-line dances and feature the closing of the line into a circle or a 'square-for-eight' forma- tion. (Brennan 1999:89)

Brennan also points out that 'until the early nineteenth century the terms jig, reel and hornpipe have been used interchangeably in Britain and Ireland as formerly none of them was a distinct form in either style or rhythm' (Brennan 1999:90). In contemporary Ireland jigs, reels and hornpipes are associated with specific rhythms, and they form by far the largest part in performances of instrumental traditional Irish music. The same point applies to performances of such music at community sessions taking place at the various locations described in this text. The remaining part of performances may include polkas (which are more common in the southwest than in other parts of Ireland), some of the less common dance types, and older Irish melodies from outside the dance tradition. The latter were passed on in Ireland as music of the peasantry when the old social order of Ireland – including the Bardic tradition – collapsed in the seventeenth century. They are nowadays included under the umbrella term 'traditional Irish music', and not all performing musicians are aware that they derive from an older stratum, which would more appropriately be termed 'art music'.

Nowadays the most common differentiated dance types and their associated rhythms are: Reels (4/4 time, but their stress may emphasise the first or third beats of a bar, depending on the melodic structure and phrasing); Jigs (the most common ones are 'double jigs' in 6/8 time; the other types are 'single jigs' ('slides') in 12/8 or 6/8 time, and 'slip jigs' ('hop jigs') in 9/8 time); Hornpipes (4/4 time, slightly slower than reels, and usually syncopated); and Polkas (2/4 or 4/4 time, faster than reels, and fairly evenly stressed). Occasionally other dance type tunes may be heard, such as Barndances (fast 4/4 time), Waltzes (3/4 time, as is universally the case), or even Strathspeys (a strongly syncopated 4/4 rhythm), or Marches (plain 4/4; marches are used to accompany some sections of ceili dances). A few traditional dances are associated with a particular tune, many are associated with a particular type of tune (e.g. jig or reel), and for some the different tune types are used interchangeably. Nevertheless the different tune types are always recognisable by their specific rhythmic structures, to which all traditional musicians adhere. It is in these specific associated rhythmic structures that Brennan locates their distinctive Irish character:

> Generally speaking, the main corpus of Irish group dance can be seen to conform to patterns found widespread in Europe. The distinctive Irish flavour accorded to all these forms derives from the accompanying dance rhythms of the reel, jig, polka, slide and hornpipe as played in Ireland, as well as the characteristic stepping patterns of the traditional dance style. (Brennan 1999:101)

Brennan is, of course, primarily concerned with the actual dances that are, or were, performed to these tune types; a question of only minor importance to my study, as the music is often performed without any dancing taking place. In fact there are many excellent traditional musicians in existence, who do not know the dances associated with these tune types. Nevertheless it became obvious during my research that an awareness of Irish dance is considerably more present at such events nowadays than it was in the 1970s. *Riverdance* and its spin-off large-scale shows in modern-style stage costumes seem to have achieved the same effect as Ó Riada's 1970s traditional musicians in evening dress: they provide an appeal that is agreeable to 'middle-class' tastes and can address the more affluent sections of society. This in turn caught the attention of the media, and consequently large sections of the population are nowadays aware of the existence of Irish dance.

Its effects also show at community level. For instance, during my fieldwork a number of regular dancing classes were held in Berlin, the best known of these by Bill Whelan's *Berlin Irish Dance Company*. *Bernard's Summer School* in Prague also focuses strongly on teaching Irish dance. Participants of such dancing classes and workshops form a part of the audiences attending traditional Irish music events at community level, and if a venue provides sufficient space they may perform a few dances during the night to the live performance of traditional music. Brennan describes modern Irish dancing as derived only from the Munster style, which is one among a number of traditional Irish dance forms:

> The Munster style forms the basis of the style used by the modern Irish dancing schools, albeit in a heightened, or as they describe it, a developed form. It also is the origin of the stepping to be seen in *Riverdance* and other stage shows since the choreographers and dancers in these shows are the product of the modern dancing schools. (Brennan 1999:65)

Of course the 1994 Eurovision Song Contest *Riverdance* performance and the subsequent popularisation of Irish dance coincided with the breakdown of the Iron Curtain and its cultural restrictions in eastern Europe. Therefore many eastern European musicians and audiences only became acquainted with 'Irish music and culture' in the post-*Riverdance* climate, and consider this modern-style dancing as 'the classic Irish dance'. Brennan quotes traditional Irish dancer Joe O'Donovan – an exponent of the old Cork style of dancing – as questioning whether these modern-style stage shows can still be described as 'traditional dance':

> … a substantial part of Irish dancing is so far removed from the traditional form that it can no longer be said to be traditional. Tourists and others watching some of these dances may well believe they are watching traditional dancing and it would be hard to blame them for this for indeed many of the dancers have the same impression. (Joe O'Donovan, *Traditional Dancing Today*, 1983, unpublished, quoted in Brennan 1999:153)

For the purpose of our study it is worth noting that the contents of the category 'traditional Irish dance' have shifted considerably over the last two decades, but their most important aspect is that the modern variant of Irish dance fulfils an important social function at larger, international meetings, such as festivals and Irish music summer schools, where it serves to bring the participants together in a convivial atmosphere.

The Musical Genre

A point relevant to all these performances – irrespective of their contexts – is that they are associated with specific playing styles. As it turned out, the community of Irish musicians at various European locations paid considerable attention to these genre-specific playing styles; so – especially for international readers – it is useful to explain what musical elements we are talking about. A point mentioned in probably all texts on the subject is that the performance of traditional Irish music focuses on the melodic line. At the perceived core of the performance are therefore the different melody instruments, which play in unison, but each one adds its instrument-specific ornamentation. This ornamentation consists of embellishment (adding of grace notes) and of melodic and micro-rhythmic variation, and such ornamentation is added and varied as spontaneous improvisation during a performance. In more recent texts about traditional

Irish music the sound has been described more expressively matching as 'heterophon' (cf. O'Flynn 2009, Williams 2010) because of its openness to micro-variations in group playing. The technique of ornamentation is slightly different for each instrument, but where ornamentation is suitable for this musical genre is taught and learnt at the point of learning to play this music. It is an essential component of the musical genre, and its essential quality is recognised by all traditional musicians.

An example of genre-specific ornamentation would look, for instance, like this:

Figure 1.1. Example of genre-specific ornamentation (Kesh Jig/first part)

Additionally, micro-rhythmic variations are employed, and the basic rhythm may be played in the range between ♪♪♪ ♪♪♪ and ♪.♪♪ ♪.♪♪ depending on the interpretation of individual tunes by individual musicians or on regional preferences. Individual tastes also determine the relative speed (a jig may, for instance, be interpreted between ♩. = 100 and ♩. = 140, with the most common interpretation ranging around ♩. = 128). Relative speed and rhythmic interpretation in performances are given by those musicians who start off a set of tunes, and session etiquette expects that during this set their interpretation will be followed by all the other participating musicians.

Irish dance tunes are made up of short parts like the one given above – often of two parts (termed 'the tune' and 'the turn'), but sometimes of more parts – which normally are each repeated. The whole tune is then also repeated in itself – usually once or twice – before it is strung onto another tune, frequently one of the same dance type. Some set dances are associated with a specific music rather than just with a tune type, and some of these have an irregular structure, or they use a combination of different tune types. If these melodies are performed they will keep this structure, even if no dancers are present. Older Irish melodies from outside the dance tradition, on the other hand, are aligned to the normal pattern of regular repeats, although their individual parts are not necessarily of equal length. The custom of stringing Irish tunes together into sets of two or three is said to originate from the early days of recordings of this music, as the length of the performance was required to fit the playing time of the record. This form is nowadays commonly used in performances of traditional music, but tunes may also be performed individually or in considerably longer combinations. Nevertheless they always follow the established pattern of repeats.

Repertoires

Dance melodies played at various European sessions were drawn from the same body of music as selections of musicians who play within comparable contexts in Ireland. Most of these melodies originate from the late eighteenth and early nineteenth centuries, the heydays of Irish community dancing, and the genre started travelling internationally as part of the 1960s folk revival. This does not mean, however, that present-day traditional musicians do not add compositions to the canon of 'traditional music', just as their ancestors did. It is their form, structure, and stylistic feel that make these compositions 'traditional Irish tunes', not from which century individual pieces originate. If they agree with the canon of the genre they will be passed on from musician to musician, within Ireland as well as internationally.

The *Kesh Jig*, which I have given above as an example, originates from the eighteenth- to nineteenth-century period and is very popular at sessions, especially at beginners' sessions, as its melody is fairly easy to remember. In session playing a few individual tunes are usually strung together, often in the order in which they were originally recorded at the beginning of the twentieth century in the first commercial recordings of this genre. Tunes and sets of tunes that I frequently encountered at sessions described in this study were, for instance: *Kesh Jig/Donnybrook Fair* (jigs), *The Wise Maid/ Rolling in the Ryegrass* (reels), *The Boys of Bluehill/Harvest Home* (hornpipes), *The Maid Behind the Bar/ Humours of Tulla* (reels), *The Dingle Regatta/O'Keefe's Slide* (slides), *Sweeney's Polka/Dennis Murphy's Polka* (polkas), *The King of the Fairies* (set dance), *The Hunt* (set dance), and a number of O'Carolan compositions, such as *Planxty Irwin, Fanny Power's, The South Wind,* and *Lord Inchiquin*. Newer items often encountered are Paddy Fahey's and Ed Reavy's compositions, and the ubiquitous slip jig, *The Butterfly,* attributed to Tommy Potts.

For limits of space I can only include here a representative selection of session repertoires. A detailed breakdown of items played at sessions in Berlin at the beginning of the twenty-first century can be found in Schiller (2004:67–77). However, such detailed information should not be necessary for this present discussion, especially since many traditional tunes are known by a number of different titles, and some traditional musicians blankly refuse to name them at all within session contexts. Adam R. Kaul (2009:144) quotes Doolin musician, Christy Barry, as commenting on a question about tune titles, 'If we start naming things around here, there could be a *row!*' (emphasis in the original). Which neatly confirms my above argument for limiting discussions of individual tune titles.

Of more relevance as regards repertoires is the socio-political aspect that 'folk music' has played a most important role in the construction of 'the national', certainly not just in Ireland. As Jan Ling notes, nineteenth-century collecting of folk music and tales played an important role in many European countries: 'The objective was to strengthen national identity and maintain freedom and independence, or to assert the strength of the nation and its ability to suppress others' (Ling 1997:15). As Ling points out in the same publication, until the mid-twentieth century folk music was collected under the auspices of official archives and by scholars, but from the 1960s folk revival onwards, musicians from various European countries started to reclaim folk music for their own purposes (Ling 1997:19–20). This point can only partly be applied as far as traditional Irish dance music is concerned. While it is undoubtedly true that the 1960s folk revival resulted in musicians reclaiming traditional folk music, the previous collecting process cannot unreservedly be ascribed to archivists and other scholars. As Breandán Breathnach (1971:117) points out, the late eighteenth- and early nineteenth-century publications of folk music collectors contained only a limited number of dance tunes (e.g. Bunting's three volumes contain less than a dozen, and the complete Petrie collection less than 300). Most of the Irish dance music was collected and published around the beginning of the twentieth century by Francis O'Neill (O'Neill 1903 contained 1850 pieces, 1100 of these dance tunes; O'Neill 1907 contained 1001 dance tunes, most of these reprints of the earlier edition). O'Neill ended his career as Chief Superintendent in the Chicago police force, and he was a dedicated amateur musician. It is his collection of dance tunes that provided inspiration for the 1960s folk revival.

Of course a musical tradition is not static, and some gradual changes have taken place since then, but O'Neill's collection of dance tunes is certainly at the core of the Irish folk music revival (see the repertoire selection above). Examples of such gradual changes would be, for instance, CCÉ's broadening views of what constitutes 'traditional instruments', or the example given by uilleann piper Robbie Hannan (1996:48–9), that in the early 1980s uilleann pipers started to adopt repertoires which were originally associated with the Donegal fiddle-playing tradition. Graeme Smith (1997) draws attention to the fact that different accordion playing styles can contribute to identity constructions of Irish emigrants – in his case two Irish accordion players living in Australia. But such stylistic specifics rather hold local/regional associations for particular musicians and certainly no overall relevance for the spread of Irish session playing at different European locations. Here, inspirational models are frequently their locally resident Irish session musicians. Even within the Irish home contexts regional styles have lost much of their importance with the twentieth-century migration to cities where session musicians from different regions mixed. And the recent increased use of the Internet has added to this trend, certainly for continental European session playing. However, individual playing styles are nevertheless highly cherished, and within European performance contexts, inspirational models are frequently their locally resident Irish session musicians.

The Instruments

Another characteristic feature of traditional Irish music is that it is associated with particular musical instruments and their timbral qualities. It is these at which we will take a detailed look now. Every traditional musical genre is associated with particular musical instruments, which are culturally considered suitable, or appropriate, for performances of this genre.[1] Ethnomusicological studies (e.g. Baily 1977, Stokes 1992, O'Keefe

[1]   Cultural ascriptions of suitability can change over time and will also be affected by availability of instruments. In the GDR Irish-type accordions were not available because of the Iron Curtain (see Chapter 5). In the northern regions of Ireland many fiddles arrived in the past with migrant workers who went seasonally to Scotland for the potato harvest. Sean Williams (2010) mentions that in the early to mid-twentieth century at American Irish expatriate dance hall events traditional Irish music was played on a variety of brass instruments because they had become easily available. This present study looks at cultural ascriptions of suitability during the first decades of the twenty-first century.

1999) have shown that there is a dynamic relationship between repertoires, styles, and technological developments of musical instruments. To understand the process of the transmission of cultural concepts through musical performance, it is therefore essential to take a detailed look at the musical instruments involved in this process. To highlight aspects of social ascriptions of 'traditionality' I have included organological details on the history of individual instruments.

The various texts on traditional Irish music that include a section on musical instruments show a considerable breadth as concerns their categories of 'traditional instruments'. While the older texts tend to include here only what are considered to be 'melody instruments', contemporary texts frequently differentiate between these and an additional category of 'accompanying instruments'. The terminologies used to denote these categories are said to refer to how particular instruments are predominantly used in performances of this musical genre, and they also reflect aspects of the status ascribed to these different instruments. Another way to describe the relationship would be to say that one or more instruments of the first category are considered essential for performances, and within this category there is indeed a large overlap between the organological sections of the different texts on this topic.

Francis O'Neill's (1913) portrait of Irish folk musicians features pipers (mostly uilleann pipers), fiddlers, harpers, fluters, and one accordionist. His selection may to a certain extent reflect the period-specific ascription of 'traditionality' to instruments. Breandán Breathnach's (1971) section on musical instruments mentions, in this order: the harp, the uilleann/union pipes, the fiddle, the flute, the whistle, and free-reed instruments (melodeon, concertina, accordion, and mouth organ).

Gabriele Haefs' (1983) study of images of Irish folk musicians in 1970s Germany lists most of these, and some additional instruments, but in a different order: uilleann pipes, harp, concertina, bodhrán, bones, accordion, banjo, guitar, fiddle (listed under the German term 'Geige'), whistles, and flute. Her order of instruments seems to be influenced by period-specific notions about 'Irishness' of these instruments in Germany. She describes, for instance, that Germans and Scandinavians often consider the bodhrán to be particularly 'traditional', because the 'term sounds traditional to them' (Haefs 1983:114–5).

Mick Moloney's (1992) discussion of Irish music sessions points out that 'traditionality' is an important notion in Irish music, which may also be associated with regional styles and repertoire. His study distinguishes 'instruments of choice' and 'accompanying instruments', and he discusses them in relation to ascribed status. At the top of his ranking order (which is extracted from an informal poll of musicians and his personal observations) he mentions the uilleann pipes, next the fiddle, and then the wooden flute. From here on, he thinks it is not possible to determine a clear hierarchy, as opinions differ. He lists the concertina and the mandolin and banjo-mandolin next, then the melodeon, button accordion and tenor banjo, and at the bottom the piano accordion, the hammered dulcimer (described as almost exclusively found in American contexts), and the tin whistle.

Moloney considers 'accompanying instruments' as 'belonging to a different category', but also as being ascribed different grades of status. At the upper end he lists the piano, the guitar, the bouzouki, and the harp; then some other long-necked lutes, like the cittern; and at the bottom the spoons, the bones, and the bodhrán. Moloney points out that this ranking order may vary considerably in relation to particular pub sessions and their performance contexts, for instance, in relation to background noise levels.

Ciarán Carson's *Pocket Guide to Irish Traditional Music* (1986) voices the opinion that 'there is no such thing as a traditional instrument', and that it depends on the musician and society whether the music produced is considered to be 'traditional'. Carson mentions an impressive selection of instruments on which 'traditional music' has been performed (including the saxophone, saz, ivy leaf, and Moog synthesiser). In his subsequent organological section he distinguishes between 'the instruments' and 'other instruments normally used'. Under the first category are described, in this order: the uilleann pipes; the fiddle; the flute; the tin whistle; free-reed instruments (button- and piano-accordion, melodeon, concertina, and mouth organ); the harp; and the bodhrán. The second category comprises: miscellaneous stringed instruments (mandolin, mandocello, bouzouki, cittern, tenor banjo, and banjo-mandolin); the guitar (discussed separately); the piano; the hammer dulcimer; the bones; and the spoons.

Dianna Boullier's (1998) publication focuses on the Northern Irish performance context, and it includes an organological section, which distinguishes between 'instruments' and 'accompaniment'. Under the first category she discusses, in this order: the fiddle, bagpipes, the tin whistle, the flute, the harp, the banjo, the hammer dulcimer, the jaw's harp, the mouth organ, the concertina, and accordions (melodeon, button- and piano-keyed accordion). Within the second category she describes: the piano, the guitar, the bouzouki (here briefly mentioning the cittern and mandola), the bodhrán, and the bones (here also mentioning spoons).

Fintan Vallely's *Companion to Irish Traditional Music* (1999:195) distinguishes between 'instruments for melody playing' and 'accompaniment instruments'. Under the first category are listed, in this order: fiddle, flute, tin whistle, uilleann pipes, accordion, concertina, melodeon, banjo, harp; and as 'less popular' mandolin and harmonica. As 'dominant' within the second category are listed: guitar, bouzouki, and piano/keyboards. Mandola and cittern are described as 'increasingly being used also', and synthesisers as 'appearing in many recordings'. Then follows a section of 'percussion', which lists drum kit and wood block for 'dance bands', and bodhrán (and sometimes bones or spoons) as used in 'other situations'. The Jew's harp is described as heard occasionally, and 'djembe (drum), tablas and ūd (lute)' as 'also creeping in'.

What becomes obvious when comparing the organological sections of these various texts is that there is a somewhat flexible, but fairly general agreement as to what constitutes essential instruments – of ascribed high status – within the present traditional performance practice, and what is considered 'melody' or 'accompaniment' seems to be culturally ascribed to the instruments, rather than musicologically grounded. To decide the order of their presentation below I have partly followed the main strands of other writers' categorisations, and partly resorted to dice, so not too much relevance should be attached to the chosen order.

The Uilleann Pipes

The uilleann pipes are not the only type of pipes used in Ireland, but they are the most common ones used for traditional Irish music, and they are certainly the type most favoured within the performance contexts where my research was carried out. Among the reasons for this preference are considerations concerning the range of pitches, timbre, volume, repertoire, style, ornamentation, cultural conventions, and overall compatibility with the requirements of these performance contexts.

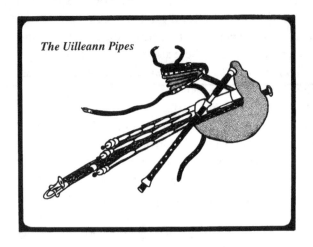

The Uilleann Pipes

Figure 1.2.

The uilleann pipes are certainly not among the instruments most frequently played in sessions. Given the difficulties involved in learning to play and to maintain the instrument, this is hardly surprising. The uilleann pipes are generally a welcome instrument in traditional music sessions, and they are certainly among the most prestigious ones. This is partly related to the fact that they are very adaptable to note-bending, and they can therefore very well produce the pitches and ornamentations associated with traditional Irish music.

Aesthetically, the instrument is considered to sound well on its own, but also to blend well with the other instruments used for performances of this musical genre. Historically, there seems to be a proliferation of different types of pipes all over Europe and the Middle Eastern world. The *Companion to Irish Traditional Music* mentions that 'some form of "pipes" has been documented as far back as 1000 BC in Syria' (Vallely 1999:14), and that the first record of some sort of 'pipe' in Ireland dates from the eleventh century. The source of this information is a description of the Fair of Carman by an eleventh-century poet, and it is also mentioned by Breathnach (1971:69), who thinks that it was a type of bagpipes such as were mentioned in the ninth century, and 'by the eleventh century pipes had spread like wildfire throughout western Europe' (1971:69). Breathnach thinks it likely that as part of this musical fashion the bagpipes also arrived in Ireland.

There seem to have been in existence different types of bagpipes, some of these congruent with, or with developments of, bagpipes used at this period in Scotland. But all these texts seem to agree that the distinctively Irish instrument known as the 'uilleann pipes' or 'union pipes', with its considerably larger range of pitches (and its requirement of a sitting position for playing the instrument) dates to around the early part of the eighteenth century (cf. Breathnach 1971:72, Carson 1986:12, Vallely 1999:410). A number of factors seem to have contributed to this development, such as the collapse of the old social order in seventeenth-century Ireland, the associated prosecutions of harpers at this period, and prohibitory statutes concerning the mouth-blown bagpipes in eighteenth-century Ireland (Vallely 1999:15,17). As a consequence, the bellows-blown uilleann pipes attracted much attention from their inception. They developed into a highly complex instrument, they assumed the reputation of a 'national instrument', and they were ascribed a considerably higher status than that previously associated with piping in Ireland, which had been seen as a rather low-profile profession (Breathnach 1971:7).

This rise in status of the instrument was reflected in folk myths, which ascribed otherworldly musical skills to musicians. In folk myths it is usually pipers, or fiddlers, who meet with fairies or other otherworldly beings, and they are often given by them gifts of musical skills or magical instruments. This status rise of the instrument also showed in constructed gender associations: the uilleann pipes were considered as 'too difficult to play' for female performers. The consequences of these gender associations can still be observed within the present performance contexts: after the learning stage of classroom-type performances, female musicians are often reluctant to bring out their pipes to perform in public.

That this gender distribution is related to cultural ascriptions shows, for instance, in the fact that there exist a considerable female proportion of Scottish Highland pipe players within society. This type of pipes is associated with pipeband performances (pipes-and-drums type performances). The instrument is equally difficult to play, but historically it has associations of family traditions. The latter is indeed often the case: female band members are often close-kin relations of male band members. But since these pipes play in different keys and styles (and partly different repertoires), they are hardly, if ever, encountered in pub session performances.

Uilleann pipes, on the other hand, are considered suitable for pub sessions, because of their softer timbre, but they come in various different keys, not all of which agree with other session instruments. The present 'concert pitch' set (pitched in D) is generally ascribed to modifications made by nineteenth-century instrument makers who emigrated to Philadelphia: the Taylor brothers (Carson 1986:13, Vallely 1999:413). Older sets of pipes may come in various lower keys, and they are frequently appreciated for their mellow tone quality, but they place restrictions on other instruments in playing together, as some of these are incompatible because of being tuned diatonically in different keys.

A full set of pipes comes nowadays with three drones and three regulators (tenor, baritone, and bass) to accompany the melody played by the chanter, and there has been much discussion about the harmonic potential of the regulators, as traditional Irish music does not tend to make use of harmonic accompaniment. Carson (1986:13) raises the interesting point that the uilleann pipes may have developed in relation to eighteenth to nineteenth-century popular pantomime and opera repertoire, for which harmonic accompaniment would have been perfectly appropriate. The publication, which gave rise to these suggestions, is O'Farrell's *Collection of National Irish Music for the Union Pipes* (published during the very last few years of the eighteenth century), which includes instructions for fully chromatic scales (Carson 1986:13). O'Farrell's first name is unknown, but Breathnach (1971:76) also refers to O'Farrell and 'his' early tutor for the instrument. As far as gender is concerned, the cover of O'Farrell's tutor depicts the author in fishnet tights and with a feathered hat; so I would suggest that the gender of the author is open to discussion.

Different types of pipes made an appearance during my research, frequently because of non-availability of original Irish instruments, since uilleann pipes are not mass produced, but constructed by individual instrument makers. A number of smaller sets of pipes can very successfully be employed to play styles and repertoires of Irish traditional music.

The Fiddle

The fiddle was by far the most often used instrument during my research. The instrument's early history is difficult to trace. Dianna Boullier mentions the 'crwyth' or 'crowd' as an ancestor of the fiddle in the British Isles (Boullier 1998:51), whereas Breandán

The Fiddle

Figure 1.3.

Breathnach mentions the 'cruit' as the ancestor of the harp (Breathnach 1971:65). In fact both points are equally valid; *The New Grove Dictionary of Musical Instruments* states that the word 'fiddle' was used to cover many different instruments from the lute family, and that it did not imply the use of a bow until this playing technique started to spread from Central Asia in the ninth century. As the *cruit* is said to have been bowed as well as plucked (the same applies, for instance, to contemporary instruments grouped together as different 'psalteries'), there are many more instruments among those contemporarily used for 'traditional' performances of Irish music, which can claim fiddle/*cruit* ancestry. The instrument nowadays known as 'the fiddle' in Irish music is, from an organological point of view, the same as 'the violin' used within the Western art music tradition, although there are some salient differences concerning playing techniques.

Boullier states that the earliest known violin was made in Italy in 1549, and that the instrument came to Ireland via Scotland around 1700 (Boullier 1998:52). According to Breathnach, the instrument emerged in Ireland in the sixteenth century, and it was already quite popular – at least around Cork – in the seventeenth century (Breathnach 1971:79).

Much has been made of the fact that present-day Irish fiddle players hold their bow in a somewhat higher position than present-day violinists, but the point rather to be made is that the bow is held in positions, which accommodate best the playing of what traditional musicians consider to agree mostly with their musical aesthetics. The physical positions of the body adapt to perform the desired stylistic specifics (cf. Blacking 1977), and the same point can be made about all instruments used in the performance of traditional Irish music, as indeed it can be made for differences between all musical genres of the world.

A part of the violin's present worldwide popularity can certainly be related to its adaptability to different pitches (including the sliding into pitches) required for various musical genres of the world. The same aspect is a relevant consideration for playing traditional Irish music, as this musical genre requires timbres and pitches that differ from those of the Western art music tradition (cf. Breathnach 1971, Henebry 1928). The instruments that can best accommodate these, are therefore likely to be ascribed a relatively high status within present traditional Irish performance contexts, and they will tend to enjoy more popularity than other instruments.

A contributory factor for the fiddle's high status is also its fairly long historical period of use for the performance of traditional Irish music. Breathnach (1971:86) mentions that well into the nineteenth century, the fiddle was almost exclusively played by male performers. But this gender association changed when the playing of violins became acceptable for female performers within the Western art music tradition (cf. Bowers & Tick 1986, Schiller 1994), which certainly contributed to the rising popularity of this instrument.

The Flute and the Whistle

The flute and the whistle are two distinct, but related, instrument types used in contemporary performances of traditional Irish music. The reason why they are grouped together under the same heading is that they have historically developed from a common ancestor instrument, but also because they are often used alternately by the same musicians – for key-related reasons – within the same performance contexts. Nevertheless each instrument has its own timbral characteristics and its specific playing techniques, and there are certainly a large number of musicians who will not switch from one to the other instrument, for whatever reasons.

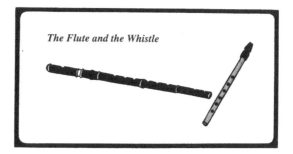

The Flute and the Whistle

Figure 1.4.

Some writers have pointed to the common ancestry of 'the flute' and 'the whistle' in Ireland (cf. Desi Wilkinson in Vallely 1999:139–40, Carson 1986:26) by mentioning older, simpler folk instruments like the *bourtry* (elder) and *fuarawn* (hogweed) flutes. As far as status is concerned, the flute is certainly culturally placed at a higher level than the whistle, as the whistle is widely regarded as a 'learning instrument'. But this conceptual hierarchy of instruments is at any time open to negotiations, as hierarchies depend also on skills of individual musicians. As the two instruments are in the Irish tradition perceived as quite different instruments, I have decided to discuss each instrument on its own.

The Flute

According to the *New Grove Dictionary of Musical Instruments* the term 'flute' is a broad generic term, which includes sideblown flutes as well as vertical and 'fipple' or 'duct' flutes – where the latter category includes all types of whistles used in present-day traditional Irish music.

The instrument known at present as 'the flute' within this musical genre is the wooden, sideblown flute, which has been developed in the eighteenth and nineteenth centuries in connection with the Western art music tradition. It seems that some instruments found their way into folk music through the introduction of the silver flute into the art music tradition (Carson 1986:26, Boullier 1998:61), which left the older, wooden instruments available for other musical genres. According to Breathnach

(1971:80) the introduction of this type of instrument into the Irish tradition at an earlier date than the eighteenth century is unlikely. As traditional music depends for its execution on note-bending techniques, the
wooden instrument with open finger holes is far more suitable for this
musical genre than the fully keyed silver flute, and this is reflected by the
fact that the latter instrument is rarely seen in traditional music. There are,
however, various types of wooden flute in use, which have additional keys
for semitones. Present-day instrument construction produces non-keyed
instruments as well as partly keyed and fully keyed instruments, and any
of these may be found in present-day traditional music sessions.

Carson (1986:26) points out that the preference of traditional musicians for the wooden flute is also influenced by its timbral qualities. He
describes its sound as 'more human' than the silver flute, and he thinks that
the instrument has in turn 'modified the music' (1986:26). He does not
give any further explanation of what he means by this remark, but it would
seem that – depending on the interpretation – the same point could be
made about more or less all instruments used in traditional Irish music; it
is certainly not a distinguishing mark of one particular instrument.

The Whistle

According to Breathnach's description whistles have indeed a very long
history in Ireland, as references to them can be found in the ancient
laws, which applied to musicians who played at fairs and public sports
(Breathnach 1971:81–2). Breathnach mentions that no details are known
about these ancient instruments, but that bone whistles from the twelfth
and thirteenth centuries have been found in Dublin during twentieth-
century archaeological excavations.

In present-day sessions a number of different makes of whistle are used.
Most of them are made from metal, and they have a fipple-like mouthpiece
(made from wood or plastic). By far the most common type of instrument
is the 'Generation' whistle. It comes in brass and nickel finishes, and it is
available in six different keys. The standard instrument used in session
performances is in the key of D, and this applies also when musicians use

other makes of instrument. Whistles in the key of D are the ones that are most suited for playing in the keys – or rather modes – in which the vast majority of Irish dance tunes are composed. Instruments in the other keys (Bb, C, Eb, F, G, and the occasionally used 'low whistle', also in D, but an octave below the standard D whistle) are used for timbral reasons, and usually only in arranged performances or recordings, as their use has to be compatible with the available pitches on the other participating instruments. Some instruments are diatonically tuned in particular keys, and the whistle – which is likewise diatonically tuned – will be chosen in agreement with the other instrument(s). As nowadays most instruments come in what is referred to as 'concert pitch', it is most often the D whistle that is used in performances.

Such pitch-related restrictions are one of the reasons why musicians who normally play other instruments, may temporarily change to a whistle. But whistles are also frequently used at a learning stage, to 'pick out' new tunes from a sheet or recording, which will later be worked out on the musicians' instruments of choice. The combination of all these qualities makes whistles and flutes very popular in present-day performances of traditional Irish music.

The Concertina

From an organological point of view a strong case could be made for discussing the concertina and the accordion under the same heading, as both instruments are closely related (e.g. as regards mechanisms for

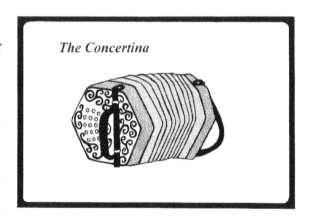

The Concertina

Figure 1.5.

sound production, but also playing styles), and they certainly have developed from a common ancestor. However, as regards their timbres, in
traditional music they are perceived as distinctly different instruments,
and also because relatively few musicians cross over to perform on both
instruments. This may be partly related to the fact that the instruments
fall into a rather high price range, and even learners' models are quite
expensive. But it is at least equally related to the fact that the button
distribution is distinctly different for the two instruments, and playing
techniques are therefore not easily transferable. All instruments from the
free-reed family have a relatively recent history in common, as this type
of instrument was only developed from the nineteenth century onwards.
The period of intense experimentation took place during the first half of
the nineteenth century, and the invention of the concertina is ascribed
to the English scientist Charles Wheatstone, who had an instrument pa-
tented by this name in 1844. According to *The New Grove Dictionary
of Musical Instruments*, both the concertina and the accordion (and
other free-reed instruments) developed from a small instrument called
aeoline (a harmonica), which was constructed in Germany by Friedrich
Buschmann in 1821/22, and which had in turn been influenced by the
introduction of the Chinese *sheng* into Europe.[2]

Parallel experimentations with an instrument called 'concertina' took
place during the first half of the nineteenth century in Germany (e.g. by
Carl Uhlig), and the long-term results were that two quite different types
of 'concertina' became standard instruments: the 'English' system (chromatic, 'double action') concertina and the 'Anglo-German', later shortened
to 'Anglo' system (diatonic, 'single action') concertina. The instrument
most often used for performances of traditional Irish music is the 'Anglo'
concertina, which is considered more suitable for the production of the
desired dance rhythms (Vallely 1999:83), and for ornamentation.

Breathnach describes that free-reed instruments were not easily accepted into the Irish tradition: because of their playing technique of

2   The Website for Boorinwood musical instruments (www.boorinwoodmusic.com)
     actually claims that concertinas and accordions were made in China for about
     1000 years before they were developed in Europe, but I could find no evidence to
     back up this claim

producing notes by pressing the appropriate buttons, they were regarded as 'easy to play'. And while they became quite popular with female performers, they acquired a relatively low status within the tradition, and they were sometimes referred to as 'women's instruments' (Breathnach 1971:86, Schiller 1994:202).

This is certainly no longer the case. During my period of fieldwork the concertina was indeed far more popular with male than with female performers, and it is also no longer regarded as a low-status instrument. But then, of course, prices have also risen considerably while the construction techniques were improved, and the result seems to indicate a reciprocal relationship between instrument status and purchasing price.

The Accordion

From an early point in its history the accordion has developed as an independent instrument, and from the experimental stages of the early nineteenth century onwards instrument makers had conceptualised an instrument rather different in purpose from the concertina. The accordion provides a fuller, chordal sound than the concertina, and Breathnach (1971:84–7) sees the instrument as a development of the melodeon, whose change in fortune was related to the spread of folk dance fashions, which required a fairly loud instrument to provide musical accompaniment for country dances.

Although accordions come in many different keys, shapes, and sizes, it is important to distinguish between two rather different types of instrument: the button

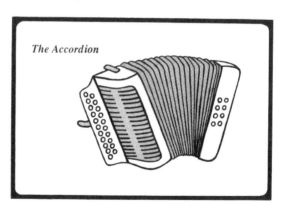

Figure 1.6.

accordion and the piano accordion. Both are used for performances of traditional Irish music, but the button accordion (see Figure 1.6) is the by far more popular instrument. In a way it can be described as 'combining the best of both worlds': it provides the 'single action' facility so valued by traditional musicians, but it contains chromatic possibilities, and its sound blends easier with other instruments than that of the piano accordion. The piano accordion is a 'double action' instrument with many chordal facilities. As these are not particularly valued by traditional musicians, the instrument is often perceived as 'large and heavy' for its limited facilities in this musical genre (cf. Carson 1986:32). The other main drawback, which is frequently criticised by session musicians, is that the instrument is often played at a too high volume, so as to drown out the sound of other participating instruments. Nevertheless it is possible to play the instrument at a soft volume, and there exist some very fine musicians who participate in sessions by playing piano accordions.

The Mandolin, Mandola, Bouzouki and Related Lute Instruments

Although historically all plucked and bowed lute instruments have developed from common ancestors, it seems justified to group the mandolin, mandola, bouzouki, and similar related instruments together into this section, although they have quite different timbres and different associated techniques for melody or chord playing. However, what unites them is that they all have courses of strings – as opposed to the fiddle and the guitar, which are discussed in separate sections.

Not all writers will agree with this approach. Carson (1986) tries to circumvent the question on categorisation by including a section of 'miscellaneous stringed instruments', although he allocates a separate section to the fiddle. Moloney (1992) includes the cittern and 'various versions of long necked mandolins' under the heading of 'accompanying instruments', but he mentions the 'mandolin' and the 'banjo-mandolin' – quite rightly, since they are melody-playing instruments – in the previous section, which he calls 'instruments of choice'. Moloney points out that the mandolin is not very popular in sessions 'because of its low volume' (Moloney 1992:196).

Carson refers to the opinion sometimes voiced among purists 'that these instruments are learning instruments', and that 'handlers of these instruments are really failed fiddlers' (Carson 1986:39). These opinions relate to concepts of 'traditionality' ascribed in the 1960s (by CCÉ and other cultural institutions) to dif-

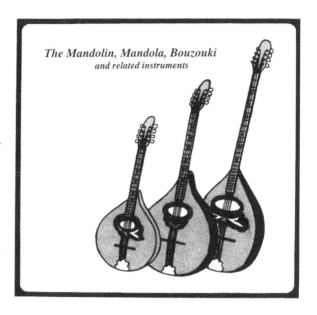

The Mandolin, Mandola, Bouzouki
and related instruments

Figure 1.7.

ferent musical instruments. These cultural constructs have since shifted, in accordance with actual performance practices. Nevertheless purists hold on to these concepts of categorisation, and they see fiddles and mandolins as belonging to different categories of instruments, depending on their ascribed 'traditionality'.

As far as the mandolin and the mandola are concerned, *The New Grove Dictionary of Musical Instruments* describes the instruments as traceable in Europe to the sixteenth century. The mandolin's modern tuning system, which is the same as that of the violin/fiddle, was developed in the eighteenth century by the Vinaccia family of Naples, in close relation to members of the violin family of instruments. It is this common tuning system that makes the instrument well suited to play traditional music, but other lutes with courses of strings also make their appearance in Irish sessions. Whether they are used as melody instruments or rather for chordal accompaniment depends mostly on the choice of individual musicians.

The Banjo

According to the
*Grove Dictionary of
Music and Musicians*
and *The New Grove
Dictionary of Musical
Instruments*, the banjo
can be traced back
at least to the seven-
teenth century, when
it was used by African
slaves on plantations
in the New World.
This strand of evi-
dence is also referred

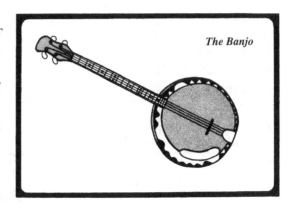

Figure 1.8.

to in Dena Epstein's study of the folk banjo in America (1975), and a
number of sources associate the instrument's introduction into the Irish
tradition with minstrelsy in the nineteenth century (cf. Boullier 1998:67,
Vallely 1999:22).

From around the beginning of the twentieth century the banjo under-
went some major transformations. While it became popular with the white
American population, it was provided with frets, it started to be mass
produced, and two distinctly different instrument types developed: the
five-string banjo, which is plucked with the fingers (or sometimes with
fingerpicks), and the four-stringed tenor banjo, which is tuned in fifths
(like the violin/fiddle, but by a fifth, or in Irish music by an octave, lower),
and which is played with a plectrum. It is this latter type of banjo that has
found its place in traditional Irish music during the twentieth century,
and its popularity is often associated with Barney McKenna's innovative
playing practices with *The Dubliners* during the 1960s. It seems that the
banjo was not easily accepted into the Irish tradition, possibly because of
its African ancestry: Francis O'Neill does not even consider it worth a comment, although it features in one of the sketches in his *Irish Minstrels and
Musicians* (1913). The sketch is referred to as a sketch of a piper (implying

that the banjo player – John Dunne – shown beside this piper – Dick
Stephenson – is not really a 'musician').

Breathnach's (1971) section on musical instruments does not make any
mention of the banjo at all. More recent texts, which include the banjo in
their instrument section, seem to locate it 'rather at the lower end of the
hierarchical ladder', regarding it as one of the 'loud instruments that can
drown out everything else'.

While I would agree that there are many session musicians who would
not welcome more than one or two banjo players at any one session, my
own observations of reactions and remarks seem to indicate that this is
more related to the timbral qualities of the banjo. As the banjo shows a
very quickly decaying envelope of sound, a banjo player will depend on
resorting to instrument-specific forms of ornamentation. As these, because of the instrument's timbral qualities, will contain a certain element
of 'percussive sound quality', it seems that a rhythmically varying overlap
of these sound qualities does not agree well with the aesthetic concepts of
traditional musicians. The banjo is not an outstandingly loud instrument,
and if such a quality is ascribed to it, then this points strongly to selective
perceptions of specific timbral qualities in sessions. Like the instruments
discussed in the previous section, the banjo is seen by purists as lacking
'traditionality', and its African ancestry has to be taken into account for
understanding these constructions of categories. As the contents of these
concepts are slightly elusive, they do not transfer well to foreign cultural
contexts, where traditional music is perceived rather by how it is performed
by Irish musicians than by elusive ideals constructed only by sections of
Irish society, and sometimes along nationalist agendas.

The Guitar

From an organological point of view the guitar belongs to the same type
of instruments as the other lute-related instruments discussed above. It
would therefore equally qualify for a claim to *cruit* or *timpán/tiompán*
ancestry. While some theories advance a connection of the guitar with
ancient Egypt, early Mesopotamia or Anatolia (cf. Buek 1926), the most

often encountered theory suggests an introduction of the instrument into medieval Europe by the Arabs (cf. *The New Grove Dictionary of Musical Instruments*).

The Guitar

Figure 1.9.

As far as the sometimes voiced opinion is concerned that the guitar is 'a newly introduced instrument of foreign origin' which, because of its chordal character, is 'unsuitable for the performance of traditional music', it is not possible to explain why the harp – which can equally be used for melody playing *or* chordal accompaniment – should be a 'typically Irish instrument', while the guitar is not. The socio-cultural background for the construction of this argument falls even stronger into relief when Breathnach's description of a historical harp is taken into consideration:

> [The 'Brian Boru Harp'] was restrung some years ago with metal strings, and sounded in the old Irish manner with long crooked nails. The sound, we are told, was extraordinarily sweet 'and clear, with a quality which was somewhat bell-like but with an added richness akin to that of the guitar'. (Breathnach 1971:66)

From this description it becomes clear that the argument about the guitar's ascribed 'unsuitability for traditional music' is a twentieth-century cultural construct. In *Ethnicity, Identity and Music* (1994) Martin Stokes describes an incident concerning traditional musicians in a Belfast GAA club. The GAA – Gaelic Athletics Association – was essentially involved in nineteenth and twentieth-century revival movements and in the construction of national identity through popular culture (cf. MacDonagh et al. 1983, Malcolm 1983, Burke 1992). There are several such clubs in Belfast, which from time to time hold traditional music events.

In the event recounted by Stokes, a guitar player is prevented from – and later physically attacked for his attempt at – participation in a session with his 'foreign' instrument (Stokes 1994:9–10). The example shows vividly how powerfully constructed images and ideologies can influence human behaviour, for instance, when they become politically charged. In the same volume Malcolm Chapman, who is concerned with European construc- tions of 'Celticity' and centre-periphery relations, describes a completely different image construction concerning the guitar:

> An unlikely combination of banjo, penny whistle, violin and acoustic guitar has come to seem, for many, to characterise Irish 'traditional' music. (Chapman 1994:38)

These two contrasting examples show that the guitar has a rather vola- tile status within traditional music contexts. It can however be used for chordal as well as for melody playing. Over the last three decades the DADGAD tuning system has become quite popular in Irish music – also in continental Europe – as it better facilitates the use of the guitar as an accompanying instrument, especially in relation to modal structures of traditional music. The tuning is also used for melody playing, but narrows the chromatic potential of the instrument. The choice of preferred tuning seems to lie with individual musicians, and the standard EADGBE tuning of the guitar is likewise used, in Ireland as well as elsewhere in Europe.

The Bodhrán

The bodhrán is another instrument that can claim ancient as well as quite recent ancestry. The instrument is a single-headed frame drum, and in Irish traditional music it is exclusively used as an accompanying instrument. Historically it is not known whether the instrument has made its way into Ireland from other – maybe Middle Eastern – cultures, or whether it de- veloped here independently. What is known is that skin trays have a long history of use within the farming context in Ireland and neighbouring cultures, and that these instruments were used for musical purposes in the annual Wren-Boy customs in Ireland. Kevin Danaher (1959:669) relates that at around the early seventeenth century the instrument was used in combination with the old Irish bagpipes to play martial music. This does not exclude the possibility that the instrument has a considerably longer history in Ireland. Lack of evidence may have resulted from it culturally not having been perceived as a 'musical instrument', especially since over the last few centuries percussion instruments were ascribed a low status within the Western art music

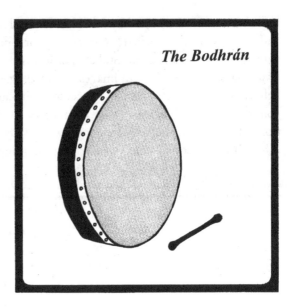

The Bodhrán

Figure 1.10.

tradition. While it is well known that the present popularity of the bodhrán is strongly associated with Seán Ó Riada's use of the instrument in the 1960s, it was indeed used – although not necessarily popular – in some areas of Ireland well before the 1950s (cf. McCrickard 1987:51, Schiller 2001:94–7). It has been suggested that the instrument may have been introduced into Ireland with other elements of the folk-play during the seventeenth to eighteenth centuries (McCrickard 1987:30).

My own research in Ireland since 1994 has shown that there may be a reciprocal relationship between the development of the bodhrán and the Lambeg drum during the nineteenth and twentieth centuries, which may have led to diametrically opposed playing styles and timbral qualities of the two instruments (cf. Schiller 2001). The Lambeg drum is a large double-headed drum, and it is not used within the traditional music contexts discussed in this book. Stylistically, developments in more recent times have resulted in bodhrán playing styles having become increasingly sophisticated, and softer in volume.

Other Instruments

There are a few other instruments that are at present in Ireland regarded as traditional instruments, but are only sporadically encountered at community music events. This applied to home contexts in Ireland as well as to the European contexts described in this study. One of these is *the harmonica*, which is remembered by older people in

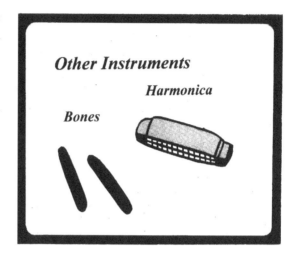

Figure 1.11.

Ireland as having been popular for playing traditional music, but nowadays very few musicians favour this instrument, although it is a flexible little free-reed instrument that can accommodate the traditional style of note-bending. Then there are of course *bones* – or occasionally *spoons* – which are often used by bodhrán players to provide an occasional change of timbre in their percussion.

The Irish *harp* is undoubtedly a traditional Irish instrument in that it has a history in Irish musical culture and it is used nowadays for playing traditional material. Although Carson (1986:37) casts doubt on this concept by stating that 'the harp is not regarded as a traditional instrument by traditional musicians; it was hardly a folk instrument anyway …', this argument sounds a bit like excluding part of Ireland's musical heritage under the heading 'your tradition, my tradition'. It seems to imply that only people of the lower classes can play 'traditional music' – which seems unlikely – or that only the core of traditional music counts as traditional music. Rather, the reason why the harp is included here only in this last section is that it is not a 'common session instrument' since it is not well suited to these community performance contexts. I do however remember distinctly an Italian harp player who regularly attended Belfast traditional pub sessions in the 1980s. During my research Irish harps made an appearance at sessions associated with summer schools in Germany and in the Czech Republic.

Another instrument that should be mentioned here is the *hammered dulcimer*, which is also not well suited for pub sessions. It is however quite frequently used for traditional Irish music within American contexts. During my research the instrument did not make any appearance, although hammered dulcimers are quite common instruments in many Balkan and Middle Eastern musical traditions.

Conclusion

In conclusion we can observe that the repertoires that feature at community music-making events in Europe strongly corresponded with those used in such contexts in Ireland in that they draw predominantly on traditional dance melodies mostly from the late eighteenth and early nineteenth centuries. As far as instrumentation is concerned, there is also a strong correspondence as regards what are considered 'appropriate traditional instruments', and instrument-specific ornamentation and playing techniques also transfer to a large extent to European performance contexts.

By following up the historical development of instruments it became obvious that not all instruments presently considered 'traditional' in Irish music-making do have indeed a long 'tradition' of use for this genre. It was their adaptability to desired style aesthetics that made them become adopted – and their 'traditionality' was then ascribed retrospectively as a 'musical quality'.

As concerns preference of instruments, in Irish home contexts as well as at continental European sessions, fiddles and flutes – and in relation to female musicians whistles – were by far the most popular instruments. However, the guitar was slightly more frequently used in most continental session contexts. This may be the result of the socio-political concept of the guitar being 'not a traditional instrument' not transferring well to foreign contexts: it does not make much sense if one is not aware of the associated ideology. Gender distribution was also very similar in Irish and in continental contexts, with approximately two thirds to one third male to female participating musicians. These figures are likely to have been influenced by urban contexts. For research in rural contexts figures for male participation might have resulted in a slightly higher percentage. In addition to musicological genre rules various associated extra-musical concepts were transmitted with the genre, which relate to spatial arrangements and what is commonly described as 'session etiquette'. The latter includes multiple socio-musical arrangements, which are described in Chapter 4.

CHAPTER 2

What Is 'Authenticity'?

In this chapter we will take a look at how the concept of 'authenticity' as a theoretical issue has been approached in academic literature of the last few decades. Although the concept of 'authenticity' is rather elusive and ambiguous, it keeps reappearing in discussions of traditional Irish music, where it is frequently charged with quite different meanings. People rarely define what 'authenticity' they refer to, taking advantage of its ambiguous meanings, but the concept undoubtedly holds relevance in traditional music circles, if only for the purpose that nobody wants to appear 'unauthentic'. So it seems a good idea to take a closer look at the different shades of meaning that can be attached to the concept of 'authenticity', and to do that it seems best to start by checking the dictionary to find out what possible meanings might be implied by the term.

The *Oxford Dictionary* provides only very sparse information that being 'authentic' defines something as 'genuine, known to be true'. The *Collins Dictionary* is considerably more specific; it provides four meanings. The first meaning indicates something 'of undisputed origin or authorship; genuine'. The second meaning relates to something that is 'trustworthy' or 'reliable'. The third meaning refers to a legal interpretation of the term, and the fourth meaning indicates a specific ending in European classical music. For practical purposes I will drop the last two as most likely to be irrelevant for interpretations of traditional Irish music. The rest of them may have had an influence on the conceptions of 'authenticity' that we are here concerned with.

The concept of 'pure' seems to have had an influence on thinking about 'authentic' music as well, since it makes its appearance in terms like 'purists'. Therefore we have something 'genuine, known to be true, of undisputed origin or authorship, trustworthy or reliable, or pure'. That gives quite a colourful variety of meanings, and it is not surprising that people go for either an ambiguous meaning or for focusing on one strand or another. Let us try to disentangle all these authenticities, which seem to hover in space and disappear every time you try to put a finger on it.

A Kaleidoscope of Authenticities

Timothy Taylor (1997:20–8) makes a brave attempt at classifying different authenticities, and he starts off by pointing out that they all have in common an assumption about 'an essential(ized), real, actual, essence'. His classification system differentiates authenticity as historical or cultural/ethnographic accuracy (a close concept to Frith's 'formal authenticity'), authenticity of positionality (ascribing race, ethnicity, or other social categories to the performer as relevant for the music), and the perception of sincerity in performances. The latter he subdivides into sincerity as credibility, being true to the emotions represented in the work, and sincerity as commitment to one's art. There are two sides to this sincerity issue: that of the perceiver and that of the perceived. The two need not necessarily be congruent. To all these categories Taylor adds authenticity as 'primality', by which he means the construction of a 'discernible connection to the timeless, the ancient, the primal, the pure, the chthonic'. He arrives at this terminology from a discussion of 'authenticity as emotionality', and he seems to understand this category in relation to the marketing of musical products, not as a discussion of possible qualities of the music. Taylor's argument focuses on the fact that this concept of 'authenticity' is used in contexts such as liner notes and catalogue descriptions to package certain types of world music as interesting for consumption. Obviously this is only one side of the coin because it circumvents the question of whether such qualities can and do exist in music.

Undoubtedly music affects mental and physical changes. In modern terms it would probably be called 'psychological' changes. If music weren't actually working to get babies to sleep we would hardly find lullabies in numerous world cultures. There exist various genres in relation to which an awareness of such 'mood changes' has been developed, for instance

Indian classical music. In ancient Ireland music was also classified along such lines of 'moods in music', into *suantraí* (music for soothing, e.g., lullabies), *geantraí* (music for celebrating and being merry), and *goltraí* (laments). How these 'mood changes' are affected through music is a different question, but there can hardly be any question whether they exist or not. So I think the point Taylor makes is that such qualities can be used in the marketing of music as 'authentic', and that this can involve invoking images of 'primality'.

Simon Frith also looks for 'authenticities' beyond the 'formal' and the 'positional', and he points out that value judgements can combine the human and the musical when 'authenticity' becomes a yardstick for measuring perceived sincerity of a performance (Frith 1996:71). Some fine descriptions how audience members judge 'sincerity of performance' in relation to Irish music are given by O'Flynn (2009); they are, however, almost exclusively concerned with stage presentations and recordings. When people ask themselves whether they find a musical message believable or not they obviously draw on the 'trustworthy or reliable' meaning of 'authenticity'. The 'undisputed origin or authorship' meaning, on the other hand, seems to be relevant for musicians in selecting their repertoires. It is not that they do not play anything 'impure', but they must hold concepts about what is 'Irish' and what is 'traditional', because they vary their repertoires according to performance contexts.

What all these 'authenticities' have in common is that they are constructed in opposition to something, something that is not 'authentic'. If all people have one nose and two ears then the nose and ears may be genuine, but they are not 'authentic'. So authenticity is a bounded category that depends for its meaning on its opposite. That is the point that Martin Stokes (1994:7) explores. For him 'authenticity' is a discursive trope employed to express to insiders and outsiders alike what is regarded as really significant about a particular music. That is likely to refer to formal authenticity, but it could be employed for other authenticities as well.

In any case Taylor's (1997) argument seems to provide a good starting point to identify the common 'authenticities' used in discussions about music. So let us look at what in music can be affected by being 'authentic' or not. Apparently it is applicable to everything: the music, its performance, the musician(s), and the performance contexts. In the music it can apply to repertoires, playing styles, and instrumentation. In performances it can apply to styles of presentation and by what the performance is surrounded. In musicians it can apply to any available socio-political category (such as race, gender, ethnicity, nationality, social class, caste, tribe affiliation), and in performance contexts it can apply to the immediate context, the wider cultural context, and to behaviour patterns of musicians and audiences. There is probably more that could be included to fit into such a flexible category, but this seems quite a workable selection of possibilities for a discussion of what people might mean by 'authenticity'.

Now how do such concepts of 'authenticity' manifest within specific contexts of traditional Irish music? Formal authenticity was clearly an issue among musicians in that there were concepts about genre rules that were observed by all participating musicians. If there is a group of long-term aficionados of any musical genre then stylistic aspects tend to transfer to the cultural contexts where these musicians meet to play this music, as Toru Mitsui (1993) has convincingly illustrated in relation to bluegrass music in Japan. As in the Japanese example the interested musicians intentionally seek out recordings, music books, specialist magazines, and, if available, musical interaction with musicians who originate from the same cultural contexts as the music they are interested in. Having said this, I should put in a qualifier, as apparently this is not *always* the case. I was given the example of Brazilian music, about which Brazilian ethnomusicologist Suzel Reily (personal communication) told me that at Samba schools in Britain often Brazilians are not actually welcome. I do not know enough about the social contexts of Samba schools in Britain to offer any explanation for this phenomenon, but it is clearly different from practices surrounding community sessions of Irish music. Irish musicians at continental European locations discussed in this study were always welcome at community events of this genre, but it is their musical knowledge that is primarily valued, not necessarily their place of birth. A skilful musician from another place of origin will be valued higher than an Irishman who is a poor musician. This is something that can be inferred from the focus of interest and musical communication taking place at sessions. Sometimes it also emerges in verbal comments like: 'Should we ask X to come and play on Friday in Y?' 'No, we need someone who has a larger repertoire/better feeling for rhythm/clearer bowing technique, etc.' But if the event in Y is a session and X happened to come along to it anyway, he would not be left out. He is welcome, but he would not be first choice as a musician just because he happened to come from any particular place.

So we can summarise that in European session contexts it is primarily formal authenticity that is relevant. At Irish sessions within their home context there are however other elements that may come into play. They can come to the fore if local sessions are romanticised in tourist advertisements as 'a taste of authentic Ireland', and musicians at these local sessions are suddenly confronted with a lot of visiting musicians from abroad who are newcomers to this genre, are unfamiliar with social and stylistic genre rules, and arrive because the session had been advertised in tourist literature as 'open to anyone'. If the local musicians feel overwhelmed by 'outsiders invading their session' they may either move somewhere else, or they may erect boundaries between 'self' and 'other' along the lines of the socio-political categories mentioned above. This applies especially to contexts that are advertised by *Bord Fáilte*, the Irish Tourist Board, as an 'authentically remote, rural, typically Irish experience' (cf. Kneafsey 2002, O'Shea 2008, Kaul 2009). I will focus on these in detail in the chapter that deals specifically with session contexts.

As far as other 'authenticities' are concerned, the continental European musicians in my study clearly held concepts about 'authentic' performance contexts, which show in the observance of 'appropriate session behaviour'. These concepts seem to have been imported from Ireland, where they are also observed in relation to the same musical genre. They are also discussed in detail in Chapter 4. And then there is 'authenticity' in its meaning of sincerity, which seems to apply to folk music generally, and it shows in the musicians taking their music seriously.

Slightly different aspects come into play when it comes to stage performances. The overriding principle is still formal 'authenticity' – that is, musical skills – but the 'authenticity' that Taylor has termed 'authenticity of positionality' also comes into play, in that musicians are confronted with classifications arising from the dominant discourse through reactions of audiences and the media with a basic message somewhere along the lines that 'authentic' Irish music is sucked in with the mother's milk in the pleasant rural remoteness of Ireland, and you learn the playing techniques

sort of instinctively in oral transmission from your grandfather. Those
images fit nicely with the nation-state ideology, with national stereotyping,
and with eighteenth-/nineteenth-century romantic ideas that have shaped
our present-day perceptions of music, and in particular folk music. Within
music-making contexts they put Irish musicians under pressure to pretend
that they have inherited their musical skills from their families if they
do not want to have their performances devalued by audiences and the
media. The same ideologies also seem to prevent local recording industries
from seeing any possibilities in marketing the multicultural cooperation of
musicians as regards traditional Irish music, although such multicultural
cooperation is nowadays typical for this genre. As Sara Cohen (1994) has
shown in relation to regional popular musical styles in northern England,
the strategies of the recording industry can be quite influential in fostering
local musical activities and regional musical styles. This option does not
seem to exist for folk music, because of its entanglement with the idea of
'nations' and 'national cultural inheritances'. And as it so happens the rural
image of Ireland fits nicely with the positional authenticity constructed by
the media for the genre of 'traditional Irish music'.

   Such considerations do not seem to be an issue for musicians to become
interested in particular musical genres, as Richard Blaustein (1993) has vividly described in the example of his own becoming involved with old-time
fiddle music in America:

> Even then [in the 1960s], I was distressed by pronouncements by kingpins of the
> urban folk music revival declaring that a performer had to be born and nurtured in
> a traditional community to be considered an authentic folk musician. The country
> fiddlers I had begun to visit and record up in western New England seemed perfectly
> happy to teach me what they knew regardless of my New York Jewish background.
> Unencumbered by purist preconceptions, they considered anyone who enjoyed and
> played old-time music to be one of their own kind. (Blaustein 1993:259)

Blaustein's essay nicely throws up in relief the academic issues of 'authenticity' as associated with bounded culture areas of the last three decades,
and it also weaves in the romantic rural/urban dichotomy of the discussion about authentic positionality of musical sources. Blaustein also
describes the normal process of musicians to become involved with any

particular genre: one hears such music somewhere, finds it attractive, searches out a bit more of it, and eventually comes to play it oneself. At that stage one starts looking for experienced musicians who play the same instrument as oneself to learn technical details and stylistic refinement. And eventually one gets to know a lot of other people who are interested in the same music. That seems to be the normal process. It is not that people say to themselves, 'I'm German/Austrian/Hungarian/American and don't like German/Austrian/Hungarian/American music; so I'll play Irish music now because Ireland seems to be a nice country'. It is nation-states that erect national boundaries, and it is the musicians who flaunt them. The nation-states may claim possession of a 'national cultural heritage', but whose music is it anyway?

Incidentally that was the topic of a conference on traditional Irish music in 1991 in Northern Ireland, the discussions of which were published in 1992 (ed. McNamee). Desi Wilkinson, a fine traditional musician himself, has a simple answer to this question: 'It belongs to anybody who wishes to play it. It's accessible to anybody who wishes to play it and to listen to it' (McNamee 1992:93). The conference was primarily concerned with issues of 'ethnicity' in the Northern Irish context and how they may relate to images associated with traditional Irish music, but Wilkinson throws in the useful observation that the 'ethnicities' of the participants of the conference cannot be placed into a single, 'ethnically pure' category either (ibid). This may have been a comment on the cross-community Northern Irish theme of that particular conference, but its meaning can certainly be extended to other contexts.

Nevertheless 'ethnicities' and 'identities' continue to appear in the anthropological and ethnomusicological literature in connection with concepts of 'authenticity', if only as classification systems to organise academic thinking. The most recent trend seems to be to ascribe the classifying processes to the people themselves, arguing along the lines that it is not the academics who construct these categories but it is the people themselves who construct boundaries. The problem with this way of thinking is that if the academic categories did not exist then the alleged construction of such boundaries could not be perceived either. So it is the academic thinking that brings them into existence. That point does not only apply to the hegemonic concept of positional authenticity but also to formal authenticity. To assume that stylistic concepts of authenticity spread out from a specific culture area (in our case Ireland) is to think exactly along those lines. The gradual transformation of traditional musical playing styles could just as well be interpreted as a two-way, or rather a multi-way, musical process (although this does not sit nicely with the nation-state ideology). As Mick Moloney (1999:125–6) has convincingly argued, the performances of 1960s/70s Irish folk musicians in America had a strong influence on the perception and evaluation of such music at home. Moloney's argument is concerned with changes rather on a larger scale, and it departs from the influences of the *Clancy Brothers and Tommy Makem*. My point here is that changes also take place on a smaller scale. Let us assume that a couple of musicians meet, say at a *fleadh* (CCÉ traditional music event) in Ireland. They get into a musical exchange at a session. Most of them are Irish, maybe from assorted counties/regions, and then there is a Finnish fiddle player and a German flute player present. The Finnish and the German musician may be there to learn how the Irish musicians are playing the music, but the Irish musicians may also in turn pick up little musical ideas from them, with none of these musicians even knowing where exactly they came from. The Irish musicians may transform these ideas, and eventually they may become tiny parts of 'the tradition'. It is a perfectly normal exchange between musicians. They are all playing the same musical genre, and they are musically communicating with each other. So how does that fit with the rather crude classification system of what is 'authentic' or not, or rather with what those people are said to perceive as authentic or not? To me it is a perfectly normal musical communication. If it is an appealing idea it will travel and will be transformed. If not it will not.

For the sake of the argument let us assume that it does. Now we bring in our classification system of 'authenticities', and ask what happens. We could use Malcolm Chapman's (1994:36) model, which allows for the contents of categories to change continuously while the categories themselves remain. That means that potentially everything is 'authentic', and the ones who do the defining are the musicians. But do the musicians categorise, and what 'authenticities' are involved? If they are just meeting in a session they may not even know whether the fiddler who played the nice little ornament(s) in 'The Pure Drop' is from Sligo, Wexford, or Helsinki. But even if they do know they cannot tell whether a specific ornament came originally from Ireland, Finland, or elsewhere. And I don't think they will care if it agrees with the genre rules. Kaul (2009) makes the same point in relation to conversations with Doolin, County Clare, musicians whom he met during his research in 2002 and 2003:

> A musician's linguistic or cultural background is not directly related to one's communicative ability as a musician in the session context. Instead, if a musician can creatively engage with the unfolding musical 'conversation' and embody the music by using spontaneous innovation in the form of varying decorations and the occasional polyphonous line while not extending the melody too far from its setting, then their performance of the music is deemed 'traditional' and 'authentic' even if they cannot speak the same language as the other players. There is also no need to dwell on ethnic, genetic, national, or cultural identities either. (Kaul 2009:145–6)

So what could potentially be affected by 'positional authenticity' is in the actual performance contexts only judged by its 'formal authenticity'. Should it travel within the musical tradition it will be accepted within the category of 'formal authenticity', and 'positional authenticity' does not come into it because nobody ever cared about it. So if we investigate this little ornament in relation to its qualities of 'positional authenticity' we are imposing our own way of thinking on a community of musicians who are said to draw these boundaries. Of course musicians are aware that a fiddle player may be from Ireland, or Finland, or from elsewhere. That may be thinking in nation-state categories, or just thinking in regional geographical categories. If he/she plays a Finnish piece in Finnish style it will be recognised as such. But that is still thinking in terms of 'formal authenticity', and I don't think it would be a good idea to impose academic categories on these musical contexts, which only appear to hold relevance for them if we create them. Worth mentioning in this context is that there exist also specific versions of tunes associated with well-known particular traditional performers, which could be said to be 'authentically played' in relation to this particular version, but our concern here is with minute ornaments that might agree generally with the musical tradition or not.

More difficult is the third type of 'authenticity' in Taylor's classification system; that is the one tied up with perceptions of sincerity in performances.

From a musician's point of view I would say that folk musicians either *are* serious about their music – and they will pay considerable attention to formal authenticity, whatever is understood by that among musicians at any specific time in history – or they will use the music to make satirical remarks about rigid classification systems. In the latter case it is still 'authentic' in that it reflects the true feelings of the musicians, but audiences will certainly perceive the difference. So that leaves the 'positional authenticity' as the odd one out as imposing sometimes incompatible categories on musicians, which are not created from within the group. Blaustein comes to a rather similar conclusion:

> If organically authentic bearers of folk tradition are willing to accept newcomers and outsiders who have come to appreciate and identify with their traditions of expressive culture, then folklorists ought to follow suit and accept the validity and legitimacy of these affinity-based relationships … they need to abandon their historical quest for the authentic and concern themselves with the actual. (Blaustein 1993:272–3)

The same point applies to the rural/urban dichotomy. It may be healthier to live in the country – which may increase the musician's vitality to play music – and it may also give you a bit more space to escape from your neighbour playing repetitive disco music records while washing his car or his dishes, but there is no logical reason whatsoever why the 'essential authenticity' of a musical genre should be lodged in the country. Naturally, regional playing styles are likely to blend in with others when musicians in cities meet regularly to play together, but this will in no way change the aesthetics of the general genre rules. So why the dichotomy? Musicians may be born in the country and move to the city, or they may be born in the city and move to the country, or they may be born in either and remain there. They may meet up somewhere, and the playing styles of the musical genre develop through what all of them are doing. *The Story of Music* (Brace 1968:48) tells a story of English 'folk or traditional songs' having been discovered by Cecil Sharp – on a fine summer's morning in 1903 – strolling in the garden of his friend, the vicar of Hambridge in Somerset, and hearing a gardener singing a song. That fits Dave Harker's ironic criticism rather well, which describes historians as 'discovering that ordinary people can talk, that they have interesting memories which can be recorded, and that they even sing' (Harker 1985:ix).

Anyway, Brace (1968) tells a charming little story, presumably for children, and since it was a love song that is mentioned in the story, it is likely to be meant to imply that the gardener – being close to nature – would know all about it. Also in relation to English folk music, Burt Feintuch (1993:190–1) describes a Northumbrian piper, Joe Hutton, who happens to be a retired shepherd, to have become 'a dream come true'. Which bears the question of *whose* dream has come true. Feintuch is not specific about this. It could not be the musicians' dream, because they had many other icons of fine musicianship before Joe Hutton became well known. It is not Joe Hutton's dream either, because Feintuch describes him as seeing the pipes as a coal miners' instrument. So the 'dream' category is constructed from the outside, either by the recording industry and the media or by academics inflating a recording industry's market success with being 'a dream come true' – or by a combination of all these. Whose dream is it? The recording industry's? The academics'? The audiences just buy the records. But how do you know whether they buy them because he is a good musician or because he is a retired shepherd? Or because the media tell them that this music is exceptionally good because it fits their categories of positional authenticity?

Now to take that to the contexts of traditional Irish music in Europe that I have looked at, I can note that there were no retired shepherds among them – neither of Irish extraction or otherwise – and that that may possibly reduce the interest of the recording industry and the media in their imagined 'authenticity'. The positionality of musicians found in actual performance contexts is perfectly normal; retired shepherds seem to be rather rare nowadays, but in any case they stick to the same genre rules as everyone else. In McNamee (1992) various excellent traditional Irish musicians from an Irish city background talk about how they came to learn their music. They all look to the same genre rules of 'formal authenticity'.

In relation to the actual situation on the ground this means that 'positional authenticity' does not exist. It is an illusionary category, imagined to exist elsewhere. However, music-making does not take place in a vacuum. It involves interaction between the musicians, their audiences, and various institutions. Now taking that back to Martin Stokes' (1994:6–7) argument that notions of authenticity are closely linked with those of ethnicity and identity, and that 'authenticity' should be seen as a discursive trope for expressing to insiders and outsiders alike that certain aspects of music are used to differentiate between 'us' and 'them', it would seem that completely different 'authenticities' are involved, depending on whether you follow up the emic or the etic perspective. This means that again we are confronted with a mismatch-of-categories situation, which is bound to lead to misunderstandings and, as Martin Stokes (1994:9–10) points out, can even lead to violent clashes when it becomes politically charged. I think the answer to the question of which side is the stronger one – the musicians or the dominant discourse of the nation-state – is self-evident. So, to put some order into all these conflicting notions of 'authenticity' held by different groups of people, I will now use a simple typology of 'authenticities' to separate conceptually what issues are most relevant for which group.

Formal Authenticity

Genre rules and playing techniques were clearly important for musicians at all community events that I attended, no matter what cultural background individual musicians came from. The only problem is that to call it observing the genre's musicological rules seems to be a much clearer expression than to call it observing formal authenticity. Moreover, none of the dictionary definitions I have quoted at the beginning of this chapter seem to fit exactly the meaning of formal authenticity. If people agree to make all traffic warning signs of a triangular shape then it is more of a cultural agreement than producing something 'genuine, known to be true, of undisputed origin or authorship, trustworthy or reliable, or pure'. Of course the music can be contrasted with other genres that obey different genre rules, just as the traffic warning signs can be contrasted with prohibitive signs, which are mostly circular. If an individual puts an oval sign on their garden gate saying 'please close the gate' then it will not be recognised as a traffic sign. The cultural conventions do not change. If oval road signs with specific instructions appear all over the country, then their perception will be integrated into the categories of cultural conventions. Neil V. Rosenberg (1993:20) makes a similar point by arguing that most folk revival music actually fits much closer with Hobsbawm and Ranger's (1983) concept of 'custom' than with their definition of 'tradition', since the genre rules are commonly open to innovation and change that is intertwined with precedent from the past. So the term 'traditional Irish music' is maybe a bit of a misnomer, but 'Irish customary music' would sound a bit funny, wouldn't it?

In any case the genre's musicological rules – although open to change over time – are most relevant to the practitioners of this music. One could say that without them 'a genre' would not exist. That makes them a handy and desirable concept for transforming them into 'positional authenticity'. The recording industry and the media therefore have a slightly different concept of 'formal authenticity', because for them the most relevant concern is that the music fits into categories that can be marketed. Nevertheless they can only market music that is there, and in the end it is the musicians who play this music. Adding to this the influence of cultural institutions concerned with the preservation of 'the pure', we end up with a bagful of individual creativity and exploration, cultural convention, inertia, bureaucratic inflexibility, nation-state ideology, innovation, and preservation, all of which are pulling on 'formal authenticity' in different directions. How this influences the musical behaviour at community level depends to a large extent on the learning processes of individuals.

Positional Authenticity

Authenticity of positionality – according to Taylor's classification system of 'authenticities' – is concerned with how the musicians fit into pre-existing social categories that are regarded as relevant for marketing any particular musical genre. So it is something that is concerned with grouping people into 'ethnic' and 'national' categories, and in the case of folk music concepts of social class also come into it, and our old friend, the rural/urban dichotomy. This means that it is important to look at who is doing the categorising, because people will have different ideas about the contents of categories. Take, for instance, the concept of 'folk' music. Not even academics among themselves agree what 'folk' music is (has it something to do with oral transmission, with recognised authorship, musical style categories, or the positionality of performers?), but everyone agrees that there is such a thing as 'folk' music. And of course they are right. If people agree that there is such a thing as folk music then there is such a thing as folk music. Bohlman (1988:87) comes up with the old quote 'I guess all songs is folk songs, never heard no horse sing 'em', often attributed to Big Bill Broonzy. Bohlman starts off his discussion by pointing out that *The New Grove Dictionary of Music and Musicians* leads one to believe that in most nations of the world musical repertoires can be divided into art music and folk music, and he then goes on to argue that such a classification system is unsuitable for many non-Western cultures (Bohlman 1988:87–90). I doubt whether such division is useful within any context, since it depends on what one sees as 'folk music', and what other categories it is contrasted with. The above quote ascribed to Big Bill Broonzy seems to call all arguments concerning 'positionality' into question. I am not happy with the labelling of music as 'folk music' either, because the term is as ambiguous as 'authenticity'. It can refer to musical styles just as much as to concepts of 'positionality'.

At least the rural/urban dichotomy has been contested far and wide in recent times as an indicator of 'authenticity', not least by excellent traditional musicians in Ireland describing themselves as coming from an urban background (cf. McNamee 1992:5, 34). A number of essays in Rosenberg (1993) raise the issue of the authors having happily participated in performing various 'folk' music genres before becoming academically involved in studying such musics. Apparently in this process some of them became aware that they did not fit the academic criteria for being the idealised pure tradition bearers ascribed to these musical genres, and that turned out as a psychological hindrance to their continuation in folk music performance. Now this is another 'bridling the horse from the tail', because academic theories are supposed to explain what actually takes place in society, not to impose criteria for categories into which real life is supposed to fit.

Because of the ambiguity of meanings 'positional authenticity' can also occur in combination with 'formal authenticity', for instance when it is used as a criticism of undesirable social behaviour. Such an incident occurred at a Berlin session at which a participating bodhrán player considered himself an essentially better musician than another present bodhrán player and consequently showed rather haughty behaviour towards this other person. This seemed to annoy the slighted person, and a comment was dropped by one of the participating Irish musicians that 'a certain number' of native Irish musicians were required to give an Irish session in Berlin 'the atmosphere of an Irish session'. To my inquiries as to why this should be so, he replied that he considered German musicians to be 'more competitive' in session playing, and that community sessions were supposed to be 'just for fun'. Now tensions between bodhrán players have also been noted to take place occasionally at Irish sessions at home; so they do not seem to be a particularly 'German' characteristic to 'spoil the fun of a session'. To me the remark seemed to have been a particular criticism of one person's behaviour, disguised as a general statement. It served as tactics to distance oneself from the quarrelling parties, while at the same time hinting at the ideals of communal session playing. Desi Wilkinson (1999:227–8) describes similar psychological strategies as being employed in Brittany's traditional music circles; so they do not seem to be unique to any specific cultural contexts.

When I later discussed this event with the above-mentioned Irish musician, he seemed to become aware that the potential meaning in his statement might be seen as relating to 'positional authenticity', and so he provided an explanation that his remark really only concerned 'formal authenticity'; that the Berlin musicians 'were playing too fast and had no feeling for the rhythm of the music'. Now this criticism could certainly be applied to some of the Berlin musicians, although a generalisation could not be justified, and neither is the same criticism unheard of in Ireland. For instance, Kaul (2009:142) quotes the Doolin musician, Christy Barry, criticising 'the younger generations' playing today as if on drugs, going 'mad-fast'. But even in Belfast I have experienced older generation musicians leaving a session over to 'those speed-mad young ones', refusing to be drawn along. In *The Fiddler of Dooney* documentary (2001), for instance, a fiddle player criticises the younger generation of traditional musicians in Ireland for exactly this shortcoming. In any case the criticism voiced by this particular Berlin Irish musician to me still seems to contain a residue of 'positional authenticity', but it would be unfair to interpret this as that being his opinion of non-Irish musicians playing Irish music, because the remark was made in a very specific context. So the meaning that seemed to me to be expressed within that context may have been influenced by stereotypical images, but its intention was to use concepts from the dominant discourse to criticise unpleasant social behaviour at a specific situation.

So to summarise, it could be said that 'positional authenticity' may be used on occasion by musicians to negotiate about problematic aspects of social behaviour. But it could not be a dominant concept in assessing musical competence in fellow musicians, because otherwise we would find ethnic divisions between different session contexts. For cultural institutions – like record companies or the media – the issue of 'ethnic' or 'national' positionality has a rather different meaning. They are interested in slotting musicians into market categories, and this process takes place within the dominant discourse.

The concept of 'authenticity' that is relevant here is a matter of labels and of compatibilities of national stereotypes in the marketing processes of this musical genre, not any qualities inherent in these musicians and their music. The two different concepts of 'positional authenticity' will of course meet when individual audience members who have absorbed specific contents of national stereotypes presented in the media, come to expect these to be qualities of the actual musicians they meet. To confuse or conflate these two different aspects of positional authenticity – its use for social tactics or for labelling – can under certain circumstances lead to absurd situations, and their effects are not restricted to relations between musicians and audience members. Anyone can fall into the trap of confusing labels with contents. Let me give you an interesting example.

A few years ago *Cairde*, a group of local Belfast traditional Irish musicians were asked to play at a concert of traditional musics at the University of Bologna in Italy. However, when the organisers of the event heard that some of us were teachers of traditional Irish music, they cancelled the engagement at the last minute because, as they formulated it, they had found out that we were not an original authentic peasant family making music together, and they had hoped for more purity and authenticity in music from the North of Ireland. At first we thought this might have been a joke, but it turned out that they had sincerely believed in this ideological construct. Sadly, we never found out if they found their desired group of authentic musical peasants.

So, to summarise this section, it can be said that 'positional authenticity' is a type of authenticity that is primarily concerned with labels. Within European contexts it featured frequently as relevant for labelling CD contents as 'Celtic music' to stress their musical 'authenticity of origination'. In the Czech Republic this aspect was additionally stressed by local musicians favouring to choose Irish language versions as names for their bands. These considerations are obviously influenced by media pressure to fit into their pre-established slots to advertise this music. How musicians negotiate around these stereotypes is described in the ethnographies in Chapter 5. From the quoted comments and dedicated activities of these musicians it will become clear, however, that by far the most relevant type of 'authenticity' within all these European contexts was 'formal authenticity'.

Authenticity as Sincerity of Performance

The third type of 'authenticity' is clearly the most difficult concept to pin down, since it is concerned essentially with the perception of one group (the musicians) by another group (audiences). How can one measure whether anyone else is sincere in their performance or not, except by pointing to a vague combination of subjective impressions? And if these subjective impressions are the yardstick, then where do they come from? If the judgement derives from musical styles and their presentation, then it is basically formal authenticity that is the criterion for this assessment. If musicians are judged by what other musical genres they play, then it is a matter of personal musical tastes, because musicians can be equally serious about their involvement in quite different musical genres. On the other hand a musician who is skilled in stage skills may give a much more 'believable' performance than a totally honest musician who lacks such skills in stage presentation. This throws up the question of what 'sincerities' are – or even can be – measured by such assessments.

Simon Frith (1996:71) gives the example of a personal uneasy feeling about Paul Simon's *Graceland* album, and he points out that such judgements are influenced by extra-musical beliefs, for instance by what he already knew about Paul Simon when he heard this music. Frith thinks it is a human as well as a musical judgement, and that it has something to do with people hearing music as being true or not to its own premises. That may well be the case, but it is still a socio-cultural judgement, not any inherent quality of the music.

Timothy Taylor (1997:22–5) extracts the concept of 'emotional experience' from Frith's (1983) *Sound Effects* to argue that 'authenticity' is relevant in so far as many people (musicians and listeners) believe in it. So to him it is 'not just a marketing tool', but something real that can transmit spiritual experiences. Taylor is primarily talking about the influence of religious genres in world music, but it is also a concept that occurs repeatedly in Frith (1996), where it is not linked to religious genres. Frith describes it as 'the ability of music to take one out of oneself' (Frith 1996:251). That is a slightly different concept of 'sincerity'; it is a comment on communication taking place through music that combines the sensual and the extra-sensual. Mark Slobin (1993) points out that this is a quality of music not frequently talked about, and I would suggest this may be so because our present culture lacks the appropriate vocabulary to discuss it in detail. It is more accessible to direct experience than to analytic academic language, but that does not make it any less real.[1] Mark Slobin (1993:106) describes it as 'the *transcendence* that live performance offers', a spiritual quality of music that, according to Slobin, is 'shared by many members of affinity groups but is not commonly mentioned in interviews …' It is actually not well accessible through the method of interviewing, but it can be observed in mental

---

1   Oliver Sacks, for instance, describes various patients with neurological 'deficits' that result in physiologically caused lack of abstract thinking, as having normal – or even enhanced – access to musical perceptions (Sacks 1985:125–42, 178–84, 1995:39–72), and one patient with *only* abstract perceptions as having equally complete and exceptional access to music (Sacks 1985:7–21). Sacks' descriptions clearly emphasise the importance of *direct experience* in these patients, and they suggest that music works indeed on a much deeper level than most of us assume.

and emotional transformations taking place in musicians and listeners. In Irish session contexts it was referred to by statements such as: 'Sometimes it really comes together. It doesn't always work, but when it does you know.' All I can say is that it *is* perceivable, but I could not ascribe it to any of the known senses, and it does 'take one out of oneself', as Frith describes it.

It would be tempting to identify this quality as something arising out of the performance situation of music-making and inter-human communication, and therefore as not residing in the music itself. But Baburao Joshi comes up with a list of other effects of music, giving the examples of 'buffaloes yielding more milk when listening to music, of fields giving bumper crops when surcharged with music, and of diseases being cured by music …' (Joshi 1963:83, also Watson 1973:106–7). Joshi does not go into a further discussion of these qualities of music, and it has not been a topic of interest to conventional ethnomusicology either, but it seems to contradict the theory that it is an extra-musical quality that arises out of performance situations. It is a different question though whether it falls under the heading of 'authenticity' – maybe in the sense of being 'genuine' as opposed to perceived 'blandness' arising out of commercialisation processes of music.

More recent discussions of the Irish traditional session context have tried to categorise this elusive quality under different labels. Some writers have linked it to the general concept of 'flow', that can apply to any social situation. Close to this definition comes the label 'craic', which Sean Williams (2010) describes as 'camaraderie' and Helen O'Shea (2008) perceives as 'joy and craic of musicians and audiences' at the sessions at *Lena's* in Feakle, County Clare. It is also sometimes spelt 'crack', as it is an anglicised Irish term of the English for 'a chat or a joke'. This comes not even close to the experience that I am referring to.

Kaul (2009:130–41) distinguishes between the multifaceted feel-good term 'craic' and the heightened state of consciousness that musicians experience when they 'lose themselves and the music itself seems to take control over the playing of it'. This description certainly comes a lot closer to the transcendental experience I have in mind. Kaul mentions the Doolin musician, Adam Shapiro, referring to the social aspects of this experience as 'the nya', which he then ironically describes as 'indescribable', while O'Flynn

(2009:194) sees 'the nya' as 'the individual timbre of singers'. Desi Wilkinson (1991), on the other hand, sees 'the nyah' as something relating to aesthetic style concepts of traditional Irish music, while Tes Slominski challenges Kaul's (2009:131) assessment that at moments of 'great craic' the 'quality of the music trumps any consideration of social status or role', by asserting that sexism and racism disproportionally prevent women, queer musicians, and musicians of colour from entering 'flow states' (Slominski 2020:24).

Some writers (O'Shea 2008, Kaul 2009) have referred to this elusive quality as 'lift', which to me sounds a bit like a key change, rather than the transcendental experience that I refer to. The closest term I can think of is *draíocht* (Ó hAllmhuráin 1998), an Irish term for natural magic, enchantment, a spell. If a medical author who happens to be a traditional Irish musician were to enter this discussion, he or she might add something about the effects of this emotive experience on alpha rhythms, but I doubt whether any of all these descriptions can help us decide if this socio-spiritual experience can be categorised as a form of 'authenticity'.

To Martin Stokes the position is clear; to him 'Authenticity is definitely not a property of music, musicians and their relations to an audience' (Stokes 1994:6–7). He sees 'authenticity' as a concept of multiple meanings that is employed by people to talk about music. This is certainly correct, if the extrasensory qualities of music are not included under the heading of 'authenticity'. They do however influence people's perception of music. They may be an elusive quality, difficult to pinpoint, but they are there nevertheless. Whether they can be explained in terms of sincerity of performance is a different question, open to discussion, but they appear to add to the multiplicity of meanings ascribed to 'authenticity', the combination of which make it desirable for the concept to maintain its ambiguity, so that it can always be redefined flexibly depending on situations and contexts.

Conclusion

So let us summarise what we have found out about the concept of 'authenticity' in relation to music-making. The first point that emerges is that the concept of 'authenticity' does not just have a multiplicity of meanings, but that these meanings vary from context to context, and that they also hold different relevance for musicians, audiences, and cultural institutions respectively. Since nobody has so far offered a clear model for classifying all these different 'authenticities', I have drawn on a number of texts – primarily Taylor 1997 – to distinguish between concepts relating to 1) 'formal authenticity', 2) 'positional authenticity', and 3) 'authenticity as sincerity of performance'.

The first of these categories was primarily of interest to musicians and aficionados of the music, while the second category was primarily of interest to people who are concerned with marketing this music, such as record companies and the media. These are the two types of 'authenticity' that are most often contrasted in the literature. The third category contains concepts of 'authenticity' that are addressed by different writers in different forms – not necessarily as self-contained categories of 'authenticity' – and it seems to be relevant primarily to musicians and audiences. It relates to a number of effects from musical interaction, and these qualities do not seem to transfer well to the process of commercialisation of music, although they are used in the advertising of certain types of world music. Unfortunately they are also not easily talked about among musicians. They seem to affect the musical experience of human beings besides through the faculty of reason. This makes them somewhat elusive for academic analysis. The example given for such situations is usually that of trying to explain to a blind man the difference between colours. It is a matter of definition whether one includes these musical and extra-musical experiences within the concept of 'authenticity' or not, but they certainly held relevance for the practitioners of traditional Irish music, although they were only indirectly referred to. They can therefore be said to be a component of what motivates people to play traditional Irish music. This contributes to explaining why informal performance contexts should be attractive to musicians and audiences, because they seem to be more conducive to such engaging and inspirational communication processes than formal performance contexts such as concerts.

CHAPTER 3

Selecting Comparative Research Locations

In this chapter I will introduce the reader to the research locations that I have selected for my comparative study and explain the reasons for doing so. My main interest was in finding out how the monumental political changes in eastern European countries during the twentieth century have influenced perceptions about Ireland, Irish music, and associated concepts of 'Celticity'. Since I had a study of grassroots music-making in mind, such as takes place at Irish traditional community sessions, my focus was on research in major cities, where a selection of such musical activities was most likely to be found.

Fortunately I had carried out previous research in Berlin, a city that has a lively Irish pub session scene, and it also provided the perfect environment for observing encounters of musicians from former East and West Berlin. My sensitivity to their nuanced identity constructions was inspired by John Borneman's *Belonging in the two Berlins* (1992), and so the theme of following along the former Iron Curtain for my research suggested itself. Normally, the end points of the Iron Curtain are associated with Stettin/Szczecin at the Baltic and Trieste at the Adriatic, with Berlin being located fairly close to its northern end. However, in Berlin I heard mention of an Irish session pub in Istanbul/Turkey, and so my research direction took a slightly eastward slant in the Balkans, so as to end at the Bosphorus instead. As it turned out, this was an interesting choice because some local musicians in Istanbul linked up with image constructions of 'the Celtic' elsewhere in Europe, and they also had quite different musical associations from those in countries along the post-socialist political fault line in Europe.

There exists, however, still an east/west dichotomy, but somewhere on the journey between Romania and Turkey the labels for the constructed opposing categories in cultural interpretations turn from 'western/capitalist' vs. 'eastern/post-socialist' into 'western/European' vs. 'eastern/oriental'.

These are, of course, crude stereotypical categories, but they remind us that music is not exempt from being classified socio-politically by groups in society who attempt to achieve specific aims by such classification and labelling. It is however musicians who play the music, and most often they have quite different ideas about their music from those of politicians and state institutions.

Where do Images Come From?

An example from the home context for politicisation of Irish music can be observed in the North, where traditional music during the time of the 'Troubles' (1970s to 1990s) was labelled by different groups as associated with the nationalist cause. Many musicians who played traditional music in Belfast sessions at this period have pointed out that by far most traditional musicians were primarily interested in this music, and had no intentions of being associated with any particular political movements (cf. Hamilton 1977, Wilkinson 1991, Dowling 2014). But then, the act of refusing to be aligned with any political image constructions is also a form of making a political statement.

Ljerka Vidić Rasmussen (1996) provides a detailed description of how pre-war Yugoslavian band *Južni Vetar* resisted different societal attempts to press them into symbolising specific desired national or ethnic images through the musicians' insistence that with their music they were transcending such categorisations. Theodore Levin (1996) dissects the example of 'fakelore' production in twentieth-century Russia, which he describes as created by 'folklore specialists' to include at least thirty percent of songs praising the Soviet political system and its economic achievements (collective farms, tractors, etc.). His descriptions provide a valuable explanation for understanding widespread mistrust and rejections of 'folklore' in various countries on the eastern side of the twentieth-century Iron Curtain.

Michael Beckerman relates people's disgust in mid-twentieth-century Czechoslovakia at folk music being seized by the political party of the day, and both, Beckerman and Judit Frigysi (in relation to the Hungarian Revival movement), describe a search of 'people on the ground' for 'the real and authentic' in folk music of their respective countries. Within the

Hungarian context this search was spearheaded in the 1970s by the Budapest group *Muzsikás,* who travelled to learn rural dance music repertoires and styles from Transylvanian village musicians, and then used it to bring it to urban events called 'Dance House' (*táncház*), inviting audience dance participation. This village dance music was totally different from repertoires played at the time on Hungarian radio, and *Muzsikás* had a huge impact in the 1970s. According to the 2014 radio documentary *Transylvanian Blues,*[1] the post-1989 period has made cross-border travel of Transylvanian music groups easier, and the 'Dance House' movement is now spreading internationally, for instance also to Slovakia, Ukraine, Japan, and America.

Within the German context, on the other hand, audience attention was more focused on the song than on instrumental music. Lutz Kirchenwitz (1993) has drawn attention to the fact that in the twentieth-century GDR – and in particular in East Berlin – Christian churches served as a meeting place for musicians and audiences who were critical of state-political propaganda. These musicians wrote their own songs, as a counterculture to the state-produced praise songs of 'national achievements'. Rüdiger Görner (2013:51) thinks that after the fall of the Berlin Wall a renewed sense of community arose on the eastern side of the former Iron Curtain from feelings of having achieved self-liberation, but in the same publication Katalin Bogyay (2013:xv) points out that all these countries that have 'shed the oppressive weight of autocratic communism' will have to work through the potential of all their cultural diversity because 'only understanding one's own culture enables to adopt pan-European identity'.

I am not sure to what extent populations in post-socialist countries aspire to adopting pan-European identities, but my point is that, although situations were certainly different in individual countries, there were certain common strands in people's perceptions of 'folk music' on the eastern side of the Iron Curtain because of these various attempts at producing state-controlled 'fakelore'.

European countries on the western side of the Iron Curtain, on the other hand, were open to cultural influences of the lure of the informal Irish pub session that started its march of success in the 1960s as a counterculture

---

1   *Transylvanian Blues*, recorded 2013, broadcast 9 August 2014, BBC Radio 4, produced by Alan Hall.

to the 'profit-driven concerns of capitalism'. As Judy Scully's (1997) analysis has pointed out, this merely shifted the profit-making from the musicians to the pub owners, but the image of the 'joyful informal music-making' is a powerful one, and it has certainly travelled to many countries as a symbol of 'present-day Irish musical culture'. In other words, what mostly seems to capture people's imagination in western countries is not primarily the music itself (although that is, of course, essential for its success), but *the way it is seen as being performed*. This explains at least partly why various extra-musical arrangements travel with the music to different countries.

To give a non-European example: Sean Williams (2006) describes Japan as having 'dozens of Irish pubs such as Murphy's, Ryan's, or Paddy's, and many of them feature Japanese musicians playing live Irish music in weekly *seisiúns*'. Williams observed many Japanese musicians as being 'well-versed in *seisiún* etiquette', and the music as evoking images of nostalgia, a 'romantic other', and links to the 'essential, Japanese aesthetic principle of unrequited longing'. Or to use political terminology: Irish sessions are an alluring image of counterculture to everyday capitalist culture experiences.

In his study of Irish/Celtic music in Brazil Caetano Maschio Santos (2020) relates that although his interest was originally drawn by personal commercial interests because of 'many Irish pubs' in his home town of Porto Alegre having no music, he soon became involved in a community of Brazilian musicians pursuing the playing of non-commercial pub sessions in Rio de Janeiro and São Paulo for the sake of learning to play stylistically 'authentic' Irish/Celtic music. Within the contexts of the eastern European newly post-socialist countries, however, the (unpaid) Irish pub session is not such an alluring image to musicians, and people's ideas of 'musical freedom' are often bound up with Jazz and other American popular genres, the access to which had been quite restricted during their socialist era. Such opinions emerged, for instance, during my fieldwork in narratives about attempts to establish Irish pubs in the late 1990s/early noughties in the north-eastern region of Germany, a part of former East Germany that lies close to the Polish border. Likewise, German musicians travelling to Poland reported unanimously that interest among Polish musicians in Irish music existed only where payment was involved. This precluded the informal session encounters on which my research was focused. This could of course change

if economic conditions should change in the future to motivate Irish musicians to relocate to Poland and bring their traditional music with them
to local community contexts. From descriptions and quotes in Chapter 5
it becomes strikingly obvious how important personal contacts with locally resident Irish musicians have been for them to become interested in
this musical genre and its community-based performance form, the 'Irish
session'. And it is these personal contacts that they describe as having led
them over time to become dedicated aficionados of Irish traditional music.

It seems most likely that also the specific effects of different types of
state-socialism have an influence on how particular aspects of 'western
culture' are received after the physical disappearance of the 'Iron Curtain'.
We can observe that further south a different image emerges. The Czech
Republic shares its present location with the region of the ancient Celtic
Hallstatt culture, and could therefore vie for being a 'genuine Celtic
country'. In fact the Czech/German border region of eastern Galicia has
a reputation for traditions of local bagpipe music, which should make traditional Irish music more easily accessible to local musical tastes. However,
influences from recent socialist bureaucracies are slow to change, and in
addition – at least in the centre of Prague – Irish pub music during my
time of research tended to align rather to images in other post-socialist
countries by favouring previously suppressed American popular musical
tastes. However, some underground strands of counterculture have persisted especially in Prague during their state-socialist period. From these has
emerged a present counterculture scene of aficionados of Irish traditional
music who meet in off-beat locations away from the centre, to play Irish
sessions that observe 'authentic session etiquette'. Personal contacts with
native Irish musicians living locally have been essential influences for these
developments, as we will see from the ethnographic details in Chapter 5.

On the opposite side of the former Iron Curtain, which was equally
home to the ancient *Hallstatt* culture, we find a rather different local Irish
music scene: Vienna displays all the hallmarks of westernised musical influences, and consequently a number of Irish session pubs exist beside
the numerous Irish theme bars catering for diverse audience interests
(sports bars, Irish disco, etc.). Even in the month of August (2007), in
the middle of the holiday season, I found a regular Irish session. For this

one the musicians – some Irish and some local – met in the 'Pickwick', an English language bookshop with small bar facilities (see Figure 5.18). Michael, who plays guitar, low whistle and sings, told me that there are many regular sessions in the wintertime (when he sometimes plays two sessions per week), that different musicians go to different sessions, but that there is an occasional overlap. When I revisited Vienna in 2017, the regular (monthly) Irish sessions had moved to *Kulturcafés* with bar facilities, and the attending musicians confirmed to me that there was indeed little, but occasional, overlap of participants. Much like the conditions of the session scene I had found in Berlin during previous research (cf. Schiller 2004), this indicates that musicians have a choice of which sessions they prefer to attend, as there are different options available.

When looking at community music-making in Vienna, another striking cultural feature jumps to attention: when walking down the pedestrian *Kärntnerstaße* in the centre of Vienna, the visitor is sure to encounter a variety of buskers of diverse musical genres and varied musical ability; some of them are clearly professional musicians. This community musical activity widely found in western countries I found almost completely lacking in post-socialist countries. For instance, many people in Prague asked me to play some Irish music in the pedestrian area, but it is not allowed. In Prague a permit is required for playing street music, which is not easily obtained, and only allowed under narrow genre restriction. So more or less the only street music one finds is the 'traditional Jazz band' playing more or less the same repertoire every day in the same spot on the Charles Bridge. A music student at Charles University Conservatory explained to me that their categories of study were limited to 'jazz' and 'classical music', that these categories still existed from the communist period, and that there were no facilities in the Czech Republic for broader musical studies. He thought that people were reluctant to experiment with new areas of study, and therefore no professional musicians in other genres could emerge from their educational system. This explains to a certain extent the genre restrictions on street music in present-day Prague.

Budapest has many pedestrian areas as well, but the only busker I encountered during my field research (in 2007) was a lone fiddler playing 'gypsy-style' influenced music in a pedestrian subway. It seems that many cultural restrictions from the socialist period linger on into the post-socialist era. At least as regards Prague, a music student confirmed these impressions by commenting to me that locally this was indeed still widely the case as regards musical/cultural developments, but they still seem to hold sway in other post-socialist countries as well, as we shall see in Chapter 5.

In Budapest I found only two Irish pubs: the *Beckett's Irish Pub & Restaurant* (see Figure 5.16), in existence since 1994, and the *Irish Cat Pub*, which followed a little later. The *Cat Pub* is tiny, has no live music what-soever, and sells Irish food and drink. The *Beckett's* is fairly big, sells Irish, Hungarian, and international food and drink, and on weekends (Friday to Sunday) they present live music on a stage. It consists, however, only of American rock and pop music, and occasionally a little Jazz, but *never* anything Irish. Staff members told me that local audiences 'had no interest in Irish music at all'. This may of course merely reflect economic interests, but needless to say, they have no interest in starting any pub sessions either. My further questioning eventually brought forth hints to some clandestine musicians privately interested in Irish music, who were however reluctant to participate in any folk music research. Given that Budapest is only at a distance of around 150 miles from Vienna, one cannot escape the conclu-sion that recent history, state propaganda, and media images must have influenced these perceptions of Irish culture.

Following the fault line of the former Iron Curtain a little further south, I had a look at the Irish pub scene in Bucharest (2012). Tourist ac-tivities seem to be concentrated on the 'Old Town' pedestrian area near the Bucharest University, where many pubs can be found, and there were indeed a few Irish pubs among them. However, their 'Irishness' consisted solely of selling Guinness and Irish whiskey, with no tacky shamrocks or leprechauns on display, but no other markers of 'Irishness' either. The only thing that distinguishes them from neighbouring pubs are the beer ad-verts: little Guinness flags. For instance, an identical pub next door, the 'Prague Pub', displays little Staropramen flags instead. All these pubs focus on the summer tourist season; they have extensive street seating, and they all have emerged in the 'Old Town' since the 1990s. Snippets of music waft through the general hubbub, mostly of 'gypsy-style' and occasionally Balkan music, and of course quite a lot of the ubiquitous American flavour. The only Irish pub with live music is *O'Hara's* (see Figure 5.17), which for a while even had Irish music for one night per week (consisting of one guy with a guitar and a microphone), but in 2012 they decided to rather have a mixed bag of music, if at all; and they certainly have no intentions to start any pub sessions.

All the more surprising it was to find that in Istanbul a regular pub session (once per week) has been going since 1999. The *James Joyce* (see Figure 5.22) opened in 1996, and it doubles as a small hotel, with advice for Irish tourists to Istanbul. It is therefore discussed as a detailed case study in Chapter 5. The pub uses Irish and Turkish decorations, it sells Irish and Turkish drinks, and apart from the Irish session night it also offers a mixed bag of live music on a small stage. Local image constructions about Ireland and Irish music are diverse and cannot be said to fall into categories of the previously described east/west dichotomy.

Indeed images of Ireland in the general population in Istanbul are rather scant, and range from 'Where are you from? Belfast? That's in Serbia, isn't it?' to 'Of course I know Ireland. There are a lot of volcanoes there, aren't there?' But on the other hand this has the advantage that national stereotyping of 'the Irish' is not much present either, and images of Ireland and Irish music can emerge from personal cultural encounters.

In recent years the ubiquitous 'Irish pubs' selling Irish drink and displaying little Guinness flags have been sprouting in Istanbul as well, especially in the university area of *Kadıköy*. But as we have seen in the examples above, they are a secondary occurrence, and they are of little consequence for our present study of Irish pub session music at different locations in Europe. So let us continue in the next chapter with our exploration of what has made the Irish pub session so attractive to musicians worldwide since the 1960s.

Conclusion

At this point we can summarise that community venues such as Irish pubs exist at all locations that this study is concerned with, but that their associations with Irish music are rather different, depending on their location.

In the East, differences to Irish music on the western side of the former Iron Curtain seem to have emerged to a large extent from a common post-socialist past. There are certain similarities in concepts about community music that appear to have carried over from their recent history. It is certain that images of Ireland in post-socialist countries will have been strongly influenced by their recent experiences of state-institutional attempts at imposing state-controlled 'fakelore' and by their limited access to western culture prior to 1989.

CHAPTER 4

The Irish Pub Session

In this chapter we will take a look at what makes the present-day Irish pub session different from other popular community music activities, and why it holds such a strong attraction for musicians from so many different countries. According to Michael Smith (1999:91), the world had more than 2000 Irish theme pubs in 1999. I have no idea how anyone would be able to arrive at a realistic estimate of how many Irish theme pubs there are in the world at any one time, but I observe that the author says 'more than 2000', which could mean any number at all, and therefore seems applicable even for 1999. New pubs open all the time, others close, some are turned into Irish theme pubs, others are converted from Irish pubs into something else.

A detailed study about stereotypical image and identity constructions in Irish bars abroad can be found in Judy Scully's (1997) essay about power structures between Irish bar keepers, patrons, and associated ethnic communities. Her study is based on forty-two Irish bars in Birmingham (UK) and Chicago (USA) in 1993/94. So the figure of 'more than 2000' Irish pubs in 1999 worldwide makes it sound like a rather low estimate.

However, my study is specifically concerned with Irish pubs where live music events take place, and in particular those where informal sessions are held regularly. Of course not even nearly all these Irish theme pubs worldwide have live music, but nevertheless it seems that session pubs have emerged as a relevant phenomenon worldwide, and as Martin Stokes (2004) neatly sums it up, 'the prevalence of ... sessions across Europe (Vallely 2003) and elsewhere (Smith 2003) created Irish bars as a global phenomenon, and not the reverse'.

Desi Wilkinson (2002:11) quotes German music promoter, Florian Fürst, as stating that in his view the Irish pub scene has made Irish music banal to the German public. However, Wilkinson differentiates between

local European musicians who are 'reflective connoisseurs of the Irish tradition' and stereotypical 'rip-roaring Irish ballad groups ... often spon-
sored by drinks companies' performing in custom built Irish theme pubs.
Criticising Irish pubs for giving traditional music a bad name has in the
twenty-first century become a truism, but especially in Ireland 'the pub'
fulfils important social functions for people to communicate with each
other, and presumably this is how traditional music landed in the pub
environment in the first place, by musicians who wanted to communicate
with each other about their music-making. The pub environment in itself
is neither good nor bad for music; it depends solely on what the musicians make of it. In Chapter 5 we will see that musicians are indeed very
choosy about the 'right' pub environment for their music-making, and it
is those local musicians seriously involved with the Irish musical tradition
that my research was concerned with. So a detailed look at this informal
music-making at locations in different countries – and in particular what
travels and how it travels – is certainly a topic with a specific focus worth
of study in itself.

Spotlighting the Research Contexts

Thomas Turino (2008:226) has observed that the term 'global' is often
used for indicating a meaning that it has natural associations with the
worldwide spreading of capitalism. He regards small-scale community
music-making as closely linked with an essential human need: that of participatory community music and dance as a component of social life. He
thinks that participatory music and dance have 'special qualities and characteristics for creating solid feelings of community and identity (Turino
2008:157), and he provides ethnographic examples of the 1950s/60s
American folk revival and of community musicians taking up the practice
of playing old-time music. Turino believes that community music-making
fulfils a significant role in community life, that there is an interactive dia-
lectical relationship between individuals and their social and physical
surroundings, realised through observable practices (2008:95), and he
reminds us that we should not forget that beyond the social aspects of

creating community and identity, music-making and dancing can be great fun (2008:99).

It so happens that there are considerable repertoire overlaps between American old-time music and traditional Irish music, but the genre aspect need not have any relevance as motivation for participating in music-making on community level. In her ethnographic study of community music within the English context of Milton Keynes, which also underlines the participatory aspect of small-scale musical activities, Ruth Finnegan (1989) has shown that any genre may inspire people to become involved in local community music-making. In this regard the essential ingredient that attracts people into playing at traditional Irish sessions is obviously its openness to participation, which is also the central theme in Turino's (2008) study. Doubtless another essential ingredient for its attraction is its musical beauty – which is, however, a matter of personal tastes.

Musical tastes are influenced in many different ways, by social, economical, or political developments, by particular wide-reaching cultural events, by trends in the media, by a multiplicity of other influences, and they certainly change over time. So let us take a look at the specific characteristics of present-day traditional Irish session playing and what makes these events different from other community music activities.

A misconception that is often heard – or implied – is that Irish community sessions are 'amateurish' events and that the musicians do not care much about what they play or how they play it. This is a complete misinterpretation of what happens at sessions, and Turino (2008:229) has pointed out that the image of such community music-making as being insignificant is at least partially created by the mass media. The Irish session is a special performance form that allows for exploring creativity in group performance while also accommodating the exchange of information about musical items and other related background information. Participants may be highly experienced musicians as well as newcomer learners, since most sessions are open to participation. Audiences may not pay very close attention to such performances, but fellow musicians certainly do. Such communication is essential to the session event because to carry on a tradition requires more than just playing the respective associated music.

Another misconception that is sometimes voiced is that by forming a circle in performance the musicians exclude their audience. If that were the case they would not choose to play in public. Rather, the explanation is very simple: a circle is the best suited formation for being able to hear your fellow musicians when playing and communicating with each other, which is quite an important aspect when trying to develop creativity in group performance. This does not mean, however, that the musicians play *for* an audience. Adam Kaul (2009:1) has very neatly described the boundaries between the session and the surrounding environment as porous, where the musical performance becomes one aspect of a larger social milieu. In other words, the musicians do not play *for* the audience, but the role of the audience is nevertheless important for the event, and it is generally expected that audiences show respect for the performance.

For this reason it makes a crucial difference whether the session musicians get paid by the publican or not, because payment implies that the music will be expected to be provided whether the audience appreciates it or not. Many session musicians object to arrangements that involve payment, and often publicans provide instead some free drink (which need not be alcoholic; quite a few musicians are teetotallers) to show their appreciation of the music. Desi Wilkinson (1991:37) makes the point that 'the drink is not free as such, it is offered in exchange for the music', but this arrangement certainly gives the musicians more power over their choices.

Both, Kaul (2009:122) and Ó hAllmhuráin (1998:189) encountered musicians who felt that arrangements of payment had a negative influence on the feel of the session. This seems very much like the Irish equivalent of what Ioannis Tsioulakis (2011a, 2011b, 2021) has described as the socio-economic difference between 'work' and 'play' for contemporary Greek Jazz musicians. The sometimes soul-destroying effects of being paid for playing to an unappreciative audience have been very intimately described by Marie Louise O'Donnell and Jonathan Henderson (2017).

The freedom for exploration of creativity in performance is undoubtedly a strong component for the attraction of traditional Irish sessions, although this aspect is shared with many other community music activities (cf. Tsioulakis 2021). However, the integration of exchanging related musical – and sometimes social – information during gaps in the actual performance event is not found in all other community music-making. In this respect the present Irish session concept is exceptionally well suited for passing on a musical tradition. In Chapter 5 we will see how important this personal communication at sessions is for all participating musicians, and that for its success Irish session music needs to remain a vernacular tradition.

Keeping this in mind, it is easy to see how these arrangements can lead to misunderstanding and disagreements between musicians and publicans. We are confronted here with a case of contested 'auditory space', a result of the fact that we hear from every direction at once, and we cannot close our ears as we can close our eyes if we want to shut out unwanted invading impressions.[1] In any case communication about music becomes impossible when background music drowns out such communication. It is therefore essential that the Irish session – whether in pubs or in other venues – is given control over 'auditory space' to accommodate this all-important communication that is an intrinsic part of the Irish session.

It is most likely that international musicians who come in this way to playing traditional Irish music will develop a close relationship of cultural intimacy to the musical genre that they are learning to share with each other. Whether they are aware of it or not: in this way they become a part of passing on the Irish musical tradition. In Chapter 5 we will see how this freedom in performance is cherished by musicians and how some of them walked away from venues because they felt their rights were not respected. Whether they see in this any 'Celtic' connections is, however, an entirely different matter, at which we will look in more detail in Chapter 6.

What became immediately obvious at all session contexts that I looked at was that extra-musical genre associations for Irish session playing were transferred and assimilated into European performance contexts. For a start, musicians always tried to form into a circle for communicating with each other during session playing. This was also the case

---

1   Incidentally this is the reason why musicians often close their eyes in performance: to stop the visual from dominating our senses.

in the Japanese contexts described by Sean Williams (2006) and within the Brazilian contexts discussed by Caetano Maschio Santos (2020). A side effect of this formation is that it displays images of an egalitarian ethos, which provides a primary attraction for drawing new musicians in to participate.

Of course even in the most welcoming sessions not all musicians are seen as 'equal'; their status within the group depends, for instance, on the length of their experience in playing this genre, their individual musical skills, and to a lesser extent on the type of instrument that they are playing. Within home contexts in Ireland they are additionally coloured by specific gender expectations, which they widely lose when the Irish session format travels to different countries. We will look at this aspect in more detail below. For the moment let us note that the displayed image of egalitarian status within the session is a strong attractor for musicians from the most diverse countries. According to Santos' (2020) description it is realised in Brazil to such an extent that all their sessions are open and welcoming to newcomers. Interestingly in Brazil the terms 'Irish music' and 'Celtic music' seem to be a synonym, which has led to a confluence of both terms into a genre of 'Irish/Celtic music'.

Home Irish sessions in County Clare, on the other hand, have been described as not so open and welcoming to newcomers (O'Shea 2008, Kaul 2009), and this certainly has resulted to a considerable extent from insensitive tourism advertising and image constructions of an 'authentic Celtic fringe'. In her description of a session at *Peppers* in Feakle, County Clare, O'Shea mentions practices of what she aptly calls 'a game of musical chairs'. It consists of the local musicians squabbling over who might be sitting where in relation to their local session set-up.

My personal session experiences in Ireland over the last four decades – rural and urban – relate mostly to Leinster and Ulster, not so much to the western seaboard; therefore pressures from tourist expectations were minimal. The sessions in continental Europe at which I looked in my study, were also very little influenced by tourism. They were frequented by committed Irish music enthusiasts who mostly met in out-of-the-way locations to further their skills and knowledge of playing Irish traditional music, and their audiences often consisted of local *aficionados* of this genre as well. They were certainly not advertised to draw in tourists interested in an 'authentic Irish experience'.[2]

Sean Williams (2010:19) thinks that the social order at sessions can depend on numerous aspects and that enjoyment of some sessions suffers from their rigid hierarchies. I can wholeheartedly agree with this description. Personalities of individual musicians are different, of course, and some session participants will always be more musically experienced than others. Social problems of contested hierarchies arise in my experience most often from some musicians regarding themselves as 'better than everybody else'. I would think that being better musicians than others would put them in a fine position to accommodate needs of others to make the communal musical performance an enjoyable event for all participants. At some sessions this is indeed the role adopted by session leaders, and on the whole these are more harmonious events for everyone.

Tes Slominski (2020) adds to this discussion that gender, race, and sexual orientation influence the construction of session hierarchies as well, and that confident playing in a session depends on feeling physically and existentially safe enough to do so. Helen O'Shea (2008) has also given her attention to unequal gender expectations within the contexts of session playing in Ireland, which she describes as having developed historically from a male discourse in relation to the rise of Irish nationalism. Although women are widely participating in present-day session playing in Ireland, the pub environment is still perceived as a 'male public space', and this can lead to women being perceived as violating 'positional authenticity' (see Chapter 2) in the session event.

O'Shea notes that women musicians have frequently reacted to these gendered expectations by playing demurely on soft, unobtrusive instruments, avoiding to assert themselves through musical leadership (2008:118). In my experience that is indeed often the case, but although many European

---

2   Such effects do undoubtedly play an important role in stage representations of Irish music in Europe. They influence the construction of national stereotypes, but these performance contexts were not included in my study. They are performances specifically *for* an audience, as opposed to community sessions. Microlevel to macrolevel relations at such events are multiple and require a different focus of analysis.

countries share the experience of gendered images having arisen out of romantic nationalisms, these associations take place mostly on an unspoken level. As such, they are not seen as aspects of 'session etiquette', and they do not transfer well to European contexts as extra-musical associations of Irish traditional music. For Europeans, the genre is seen as 'folk music' and therefore as not carrying any ascriptions of being a 'male genre'. Also, pubs on the continent are frequently more openly spaced than pubs in Ireland, and many sessions took place in cultural venues, rather than in pubs. For my research the option of remaining unobtrusively in the background where this was the most effective strategy proved an advantage because I saw my role as finding out what musicians at these European locations were doing with Irish traditional music by affecting as little change as possible by my participation.

What all these examples show is that the egalitarian ethos of the session is not always easily reconcilable with individual bias, social pressures, and competition for status within the group. They can even become distinctly unpleasant and dangerous when they occur within politically charged contexts, such as the one described by Martin Stokes (1994:9–10) in Northern Ireland, which led to physical harm over contested session participation (see also the discussion of the contested status of the guitar in Chapter 1).

Fortunately a friendly egalitarian ethos was widely prevalent at the European sessions that I attended. The main reasons for establishing hierarchies was length of experience in playing this genre. Newcomers will frequently need some time to absorb the unspoken rules usually referred to as 'session etiquette'. They relate to such socio-musical aspects as always observing mutual respect for fellow musicians, to follow the lead of whoever starts playing any particular set of tunes, and preserving a harmonious group performance by not overpowering contributions of other musicians. They can best be described as a multifaceted combination of social skills, group awareness, and feeling for the *draíocht* of the music. Even at home in Ireland some musicians are more skilled in accommodating these than others.

In other words: passing on a musical tradition requires learning on many different levels. In any case it can be observed that the circular formation for exploring creativity in group performance is nowadays very much a cultural trait of traditional Irish community music-making. This feature came strikingly to the fore in an intercultural ensemble collaboration project between professional traditional Irish and Senegalese musicians in 2002, described by Desi Wilkinson (2011). The four Irish and four Senegalese musicians were given five days at a pleasant northern Irish retreat to explore a cross-cultural compositional project that was to be presented at two subsequent local concerts. The Irish musicians approached the task by intuitively forming a loose circle with acoustic instruments, while the Senegalese musicians started off by being plugged into a fully set up sound system. Wilkinson explains how this came about by the Senegalese musicians being used to the dominant tradition for 'World Music', which at present is the Western rock idiom. In the event the Irish musicians – being the host – adjusted to the visitors, but my point in this context is that in the twentieth century traditional Irish music within informal contexts has inextricably become linked with forming a loose circle for exploring creativity in group performance.

Figure 4.1. The typical circular formation of the traditional Irish session.
This photograph was taken in 2001 at the *Cliffs of Dunneen* session in Berlin.

Conclusion

It can be said in conclusion that Irish session playing involves a variety of socio-musical cultural intimacies, but that it is its specific group formation that facilitates communication in improvisational group performance and exudes egalitarian inclusiveness, which has undoubtedly added attractiveness for many musicians worldwide. The combination of these specific musical and extra-musical associations for Irish traditional music have proven most attractive for musicians from many different cultural backgrounds, which suggests that it fulfils an important need in contemporary European society.

CHAPTER 5

Creating Meaning through Music at Different Locations

A Selection of Ethnographic Case Studies

Martin Stokes is certainly not the only ethnomusicologist who has stressed the importance of a detailed ethnography (cf. Finnegan 1989, Stokes 1994, 2010, Tsioulakis 2011a, 2011b, 2021) for understanding people's community music activities. Therefore in this chapter I will try to make sense of what people do with Irish traditional music at different locations by looking at their musical practices through a magnifying lens.

There are different approaches possible for an ethnographer to study a particular slice of the musical multiplicity of this world. For instance, one can use a diachronic approach by closely following a particular musical genre over time, or one can choose a synchronic approach by focusing on a specified moment in time. Ruth Finnegan (1989) has chosen for her study to look at all musical genres she found observable at one particular location (Milton Keynes) at a specific point in time. For my study I have chosen the genre (traditional Irish music) as the unifying factor, to compare its use at different European locations. Also, my time frame is a little more flexible, as I have returned to fieldwork locations at different times, so as to look at developments of community music activities. And again I agree with Stokes (1994, but see also Seeger 1977) that such music-making is a flexible and fluid activity that creates and changes, contests and negotiates, musical meanings within specific contexts.

Of course, even a 'slice' of Europe from the Baltic to the Mediterranean is a big place, and by looking in detail at an Irish music summer school in Prague I may have missed a community Irish music festival taking place at the same time in Vienna. Clearly it is impossible to provide an all-inclusive overview of even one genre for such a large area. What I am providing here are enlargements of snapshots from my chosen area of research. Hopefully they will encourage new ways of thinking about the role of traditional Irish music in community music-making at different locations. After all, there is no reason why Irish music should only travel to the traditional Irish emigration destinations of England, America, and Australia, since an instrumental musical genre can easily travel across language barriers.[1]

Certainly there are always Irish musicians who claim that 'the pure drop needs to be sucked in through the home soil', but many musicians are more interested in music than in politics (see Chapter 3), and therefore the argument that one context might be more 'authentic' than another seems rather futile, especially since 'authenticity' is such a flexible concept. I will, however, pay attention what concepts of 'authenticity' are invoked where I have looked in detail at communications between musicians from Ireland with musicians from various other places of the world, hoping that in the process we will see connections of how the local links with the global.

Irish Music in Berlin

The first place I looked at as part of my journey along the former Iron Curtain was Berlin. Located at a historically significant intersection of East and West (cf. Schiller 2004), I could fall back on previous contacts I had made with Irish traditional musicians living in this city. In Berlin I had discovered a variety of Irish community session events at which people from Germany, Ireland, England, Scotland, Austria, Switzerland, America, Russia, Hungary, and occasionally some other countries

---

1   I should add here a note on language. Conversations with musicians were conducted in multiple languages, often simultaneously, because all of us were drawing on multilingual expressions to communicate meanings. However, I wrote down my field notes in English. For finding out how people came to Irish music I used mini questionnaires in their local languages. Their responses overwhelmingly confirmed the essential relevance of personal contacts with local Irish musicians.

participated. Of course, from the 'Cold War' days Berlin is a melting pot of people from many different cultural backgrounds, but as we shall see later, such a multicultural mix of participants is not unusual at any one location. It is the musical genre that draws musicians in, and most often there are one or two Irish-born musicians who have established the session and who have kept it going over years. Where such a connection with Irish music has been established for many years, skilled local musicians may take up the teaching of the techniques for traditional Irish music to beginners, thereby contributing to the continuation of a local tradition. Especially summer schools for Irish music – such as the annual German event at Proitzer Mühle near Lüneburg in June, or Bernard's Summer School taking place every year in August in Prague – employ local teachers besides those invited over from Ireland for teaching instrument techniques on various levels of proficiency.

Fintan Vallely (1998:39–40) has argued for 'audible ethnicity' in the playing of Irish music, especially in the case of German and French musicians, but during my fieldwork this image proved unfounded. Of course a classical musician trying to learn to play traditional music will sound like a classical musician learning to play traditional music, but this will equally apply to German, French, or Irish musicians. Each genre has its own stylistic aesthetics.

To test whether my hearing might be biased I carried out a test at a Queen's University Belfast postgraduate seminar attended by students from a variety of cultural backgrounds.

As part of my presentation I played three musical examples recorded at different session performances, and all examples consisted of the same type of dance tunes (reels). One example was recorded at a local Belfast session, one example was recorded at a Berlin session of only German musicians, and the third example was recorded at a Berlin session attended by a combination of Irish and non-Irish musicians. I gave out mini questionnaires, and I asked the students to mark which of the performances they associated with which location and which composition of musicians. The resulting answers were quite arbitrary and showed all different combinations of possibilities. When discussing their answers afterwards, one student had identified the same fiddle player who featured on two of the tracks as 'German-sounding' in one example and as 'Irish-sounding' in the other. Another student thought that one of the performances 'sounded faster', and that this seemed to indicate an Irish context. Actually the local Belfast performance was the slowest of all examples, although the speed was rather similar in all examples. Significantly, quite a few of the participants related that they had 'just guessed' because they could not hear any 'Irish' or 'non-Irish' differences.

Possible conclusions from this test are that there exist certain cultural associations in people's minds, which influence their forming of opinions. If the musical performances do not fall into clearly established categories, the listener tries to associate perceived differences with possible categories. In other words, the analytical mind interprets casual differences that can be observed between any two performances (for instance induced by the weather, or by the mood of the publican), as possibly holding relevance for 'ethnic' differences. This suggests the far more likely conclusion that any perceived differences hold no relevance for stylistically trying to classify people and their performances into 'ethnic groups', and that the concept of 'audible ethnicity' is an invented cultural construct that does not bear out at actual music-making events. This does not mean, however, that the concept of genetically inherited musical playing styles does not exist within society. In fact such concepts exist within many societies worldwide, and they may be ascribed to a specific gender, caste, religion, occupational group, or as the case may be, to 'audible ethnicity'.

In *The Making of Irish Traditional Music* (2008:96–7) Helen O'Shea refers to the concept of audible ethnicity as reproducing 'the longstanding stereotype of the foreign tourist, usually German or French, who earnestly attempts to adopt Irish ways, to the amusement and contempt of the "locals"'. She gives two anecdotal examples, in the first of which the 'locals' are making fun of a visiting musician known to be German, while in the second example the 'locals' admire the great playing skills of some visiting musicians, of whom they only find out in retrospect that they are from France. Her examples prove my point that 'audible ethnicity' is a social construct with no basis in the quality of the music being played.

So we can start our detailed look at the Berlin Irish session scene by keeping in mind that the actual music sounds much the same as at sessions within the home context. However, there were other differences, and it was most fortunate that I had chosen the Irish music scene in Berlin as a starting point for my project, because at this location on the cusp between eastern and western Europe it became very soon apparent that, although the Wall had at this time physically disappeared, musicians from the former East and West saw the genre of traditional Irish music – and by extension the whole wider field of Irish culture – with different eyes. The Iron Curtain had not just kept *people* apart, but also their access to each other's culture. As can be expected, this had wide-reaching consequences.

Many – indeed nearly all – Irish records, books, films etc. had not been available on the Eastern side before the 1990s, the English language was not taught in schools (as it was in the West), and even musical instruments – such as were available – were technologically constructed for different genres and often not suited for playing traditional Irish music in the same styles and keys as it is played in Ireland.

Western radio and television stations were receivable on the Eastern side, but it was *verboten* to listen to these, and trespassing could land one in prison, or worse. Eastern radio and television stations were available on the Western side, but East German merchandise – like records, books, films, etc. – mostly not, and many items were forbidden to be exported. In this age of Internet transparency it seems difficult to imagine how such a cultural embargo could have been so effective, but it certainly was, and the fallout of related culture-specific colourings showed within the informal performance contexts of traditional Irish music in Berlin.

Of course at the time that I carried out my research, the actual Wall had disappeared, but culturally constructed images have a tendency to linger on, although they may not be immediately apparent. In *Belonging in the two Berlins* (1992), John Borneman's ethnosemantic approach to interview analysis relates that his interviewees used different – and frequently not value-free – terminology to describe historical events, depending on which side of the Wall they had been living at before the Wall came down. This is a very fine example to show that culture-specific images of Ireland will not change overnight, and neither will images of traditional Irish music.

To understand the current attraction of sessions in Berlin, we have to take into consideration the statements of many musicians that since the fall of the Wall folk music venues in Berlin have rapidly disappeared. Low-budget premises in former back streets facing the Wall were more or less overnight catapulted into fashionable areas, and consequently they steeply rose in expenses. This spelt an end to their small-scale stage events, and so meeting at sessions became important for musicians to keep in contact with each other musically.[2]

In the early twenty-first century there were a number of community pubs where musicians met for sessions. For instance, once per week musicians met in the *Emerald Isle* (see Figure 5.2), which is situated in *Berlin-Kreuzberg* (in the former West), and once per week musicians met in a pub called *Cliffs of Dunneen* (see Figure 4.1), situated in *Berlin-Prenzlauerberg* (in the former East). Both these pubs are under German management. Uilleann piper Christian Tschirch was one of the main musicians who played in the *Emerald Isle* session, but he also occasionally attended the other weekly session in the *Cliffs of Dunneen*, which takes place on a different night of the week. Some other musicians, like Walter Bracht, also used to go to both sessions, but they do not always have the time to do so. Session musicians change their attendance patterns over time, and it is not possible to predict who will attend which session. Some musicians are teachers and only show up during school holidays. Some musicians attend sessions because they are in Berlin temporarily (for study, work, research, whatever); others come because it is next door to where they are living and the session playing keeps them in touch with the Irish music community. And, of course, individuals may have multiple and/or varying reasons for attending sessions.

The *Cliffs of Dunneen* is a small community pub with six tables, attended by local working class clientele during the week, and offering a venue for Irish musicians on Sundays. The *Cliffs of Dunneen* session had been started in the 1990s by a few musicians living nearby. Their 'resident piper' used to be Dave Bradfield, who came to Berlin in 1981 from Co. West Meath. Dave started to learn playing the pipes in Berlin in the 1980s, and

---

2   Even worse affected by the fall of the Wall were classical musicians, because the Eastern and Western orchestras were soon amalgamated into one. As a consequence many classical musicians lost their employment.

he worked on various other cultural projects connected with Ireland. None of them provided sufficient money to live on, and after losing out on them repeatedly Dave curtailed his focus on music and started to concentrate on his travelling workshops of teaching *Shiatsu* massage.

Dave's *Meeting Place*, renamed as *Tír na nÓg Irish Celtic Craft and Music Shop* (see Plate 2) should also be mentioned as a session venue. It has closed by now (since 2004), but it existed for about two decades, and it was still in existence during the early stages of my fieldwork. From the 1990s onwards, the *Meeting Place/Tír na nÓg* was probably best known in its function as a music shop (see Figure 5.1), selling Irish and other folk music instruments and musical paraphernalia, but it served also for some other purposes. According to Dave's description, he already had in mind different activities when he set up the *Meeting Place* in the 1980s. He required the place for teaching Shiatsu, but he also wanted it to be a place to 'give people somewhere else to play this [traditional Irish] music besides in pubs'. As it turned out it was additionally used for tin whistle classes and tuition for some other instruments, and for Irish language classes (attended by Irish and German people). Besides that Dave was repairing musical instruments, and so musicians often came into the shop; either for having instruments repaired, or for buying musical instruments or paraphernalia, or for spontaneous playing of music with whoever was present at the time. In the 1990s some of these musicians formed themselves into *The Tír na nÓg Session Band*, who also played in various other venues in Berlin. Dave played with this group, and he described the members of this band as 'a loose connection of musicians, including Peter O'Callaghan, Walter Bracht, Bob Campbell from Australia, and Alberto, a Spanish flute player'. The *Meeting Place/Tír na nÓg* may not have been a big session venue, but it was there for a long time. And since it resulted in the forming of a band it can certainly be said to have been relevant for session musicians.

Also worth mentioning in relation to session playing is Dave Bradfield's *May Fleadh Cheoil*, which was an annual community festival organised by Dave. It took place every year on the First of May in the large grassy yard behind his shop, and it continued for a while even after the shop had closed. People from the local neighbourhood had come to appreciate it over the years, and they asked Dave to continue it, despite the disappearance of the shop. No one had to pay in, and no one received payment for anything either. It included session playing of traditional Irish music and Irish dance exhibitions, and it was attended by Irish and German Berlin residents, as well as by people from other countries of origin interested in Irish culture. It was a meeting occasion for many of the musicians from the Berlin Irish music scene. They showed up at whatever time their personal circumstances permitted, and when present they partook in the session. It was not unusual that there were about twenty musicians playing simultaneously, and most of them were professionals or semi-professionals. But this was not a condition for playing; whoever attended was invited to participate.

But to return to the session pubs: apart from the *Emerald Isle* and the *Cliffs of Dunneen*, there were at the time two other Irish pubs in existence which had occasional sessions: one in *Berlin-Kreuzberg* and one in

Figure 5.1. Dave Bradfield in his *Tír na nÓg* Celtic craft and music shop in Berlin-Kreuzberg

Figure 5.2. Irish session at the *Emerald Isle* pub in Berlin-Kreuzberg

Berlin-Neukölln; both being working-class districts of former West Berlin, with a fairly large international composition of residents. The *Blarney Pub* session was organised on a monthly basis by German fiddle player, Wolfgang Bathke (see Figure 5.3). With its publican and bar staff from Ireland, this session was frequented by a fairly equal distribution of Irish and German musicians. Some of them also play together on a professional basis, as for instance Aaron Shirlow, Noel Minogue, and Bernd Lüdtke in the group *Midnight Court*. Quite a few of the other participants attended both, the *Emerald Isle* and the *Cliffs of Dunneen* sessions.

The other session pub, the *Molly Malone's* (see Figure 5.4), also owned by an Irishman, had only just started having events in 2003, and was attended by musicians who were mostly newcomers to playing this music in sessions: they had come to this genre through dance. They brought their own CDs with them, to which they did their dancing in between their session playing.

In 2006 the *Molly Malone's* pub moved to *Berlin-Wilmersdorf*, a slightly leafier area of Berlin – to a pub with a small beer garden, and the dancers moved with them. The *Molly Malone's* staff team was quite

Figure 5.3. Irish session at the *Blarney Pub* in Berlin-Kreuzberg; the author plays the mandolin.

international: Marcus himself is from Dublin, his waitresses were from Germany and Hungary, and his chef was Italian. The dancers/musicians were mostly from former East Berlin, but by 2009 also musicians from the other session pubs occasionally attended the *Molly Malone's* session. By popular demand Marcus started weekly instrumental music classes in the pub, and he also added other cultural events to present different aspects of Irish culture to his patrons. All went well until one of his neighbours started to imagine that Irish music played on small acoustic instruments was particularly loud. This was all the more surprising since there were a train line and a motorway running by right next door.

Although the *Molly Malone's* had additional sound proofing installed, their neighbour kept complaining about 'excessively loud music', until in 2016 Marcus decided to sell up, hold a big farewell party for all his Berlin friends, and to move back to Ireland. It is a sad end to a lovely Irish project in Berlin. Of course the musicians can meet at the other Berlin session pubs, but the dancers will need to find a new home.

Figure 5.4. Irish session at the *Molly Malone's* pub in Berlin-Wilmersdorf. Publican Marcus Bland looks on, enjoying the music.

What is interesting about Berlin Irish sessions is that there was very little genre mixing except for occasional contributions of English or Scottish folk songs, which are regarded as 'close cousin' genres much like in Ireland. But despite close proximity of Turkish folk music in Berlin, and musicians' awareness of genre similarities in that both use no harmonies, but extensive micro-ornamentation of the melodic line, Middle Eastern music made only one appearance during my time of research. It happened at the *Blarney Pub*, at around 3 a.m., when the Irish session proper was over, but a few musicians still lingered on, playing bits and pieces of various origin for fun in an almost empty pub, at which myself and a resident Scottish musician contributed Greek-Turkish instrumental pieces. The other musicians didn't join in and laughingly commented that apparently 'we both had caught that bug'. This allows for the inference that such music does not normally make an appearance at Berlin Irish sessions, even if they take place in *Kreuzberg*, which is internationally known for its large percentage of Turkish residents.

In this context it is interesting to bear in mind that Berlin Irish sessions are frequently attended by diverse international – not just western – musicians with a common interest and long-term dedication to Irish music. For instance, in July 2019 at the monthly *Blarney Pub* session three musicians turned up who had come together because of their common interest in Irish music. One of them was a fiddle player from Israel, one was a fiddle player from Iran, and one was a guitarist from Turkey. The latter, Cem, told me that when living in Istanbul a few years previously he had attended the local Irish session in the *James Joyce Pub* (discussed in detail in the section of Irish music in Istanbul). This certainly shows that Irish music communities in Europe are not diasporic communities as such, and that participants may meet up again over time within different international Irish music contexts, which underlines their long-term dedication to this genre.

As far as Irish dancing in Germany is concerned, it did not attract much attention during the 1960s/70s folk revival; it seems to have arrived in Berlin session pubs only after the 1989 fall of the Wall, with the 1990s dance craze initiated by the *Riverdance* success. But the playing of the music was there first; so it is not that people have started to play the music to please the dancers. The two interests seem to develop rather independently, and every now and then they meet, for instance also spontaneously when dancers are present at small-scale community Irish music stage events.

Apart from these community venues, there are also quite a few stereotypical 'Irish pubs' on, or near, the main tourist boulevards, which restrict their cultural offers more or less to Irish beverages, addressing primarily passing tourist audiences. What is most interesting and telling is that the local Germans actually use different terminology for these types of pub. The touristy chain Irish pubs are called *Irish Pubs*, whereas the neighbourhood pubs where musicians and local audiences meet and communicate with each other, are referred to as *irische Kneipen* – which is, of course, German for 'Irish pubs', but the use of native language expresses that these community pubs occupy a different status in the perception of local musicians and audiences.

So we can summarise that Berlin has a lively community Irish music scene, with quite a few session pubs frequented by partially overlapping groups of musicians. These sessions are open for participation. However, status is ascribed not only according to the quality of musical performance, but also in relation to how long individual musicians have been involved with this musical genre. Not surprisingly, these two aspects are often directly related to each other, but as far as session playing is concerned, musicians from the former GDR are at a disadvantage because even informal get-togethers in local pubs for Irish session playing were strictly forbidden in the GDR. So before the fall of the Wall their 'session playing' consisted of occasionally meeting up at private parties to exchange a few Irish tunes. Therefore going to local pubs to play traditional Irish music with other musicians was quite a new experience to them in the 1990s. In this process they learned new cultural concepts associated with this genre that had hitherto been inaccessible to them, and of course they discovered also other aspects of Irish culture.

In the context of these discoveries, an interesting aspect in session playing came to the surface as regards accordions. These free-reed instruments come in different sizes, with piano-type keys or with buttons, and some are diatonically tuned to different keys, while others are chromatically tuned. Traditional Irish music, however, is played in specific keys that are compatible with all instruments that are regarded as traditional for this genre, and not all types of accordion meet this requirement. So after the fall of the Wall, GDR musicians found themselves affected by a legacy they had not chosen. This legacy stems from socio-economic conditions in the GDR, under which decisions on instrument construction were not made – nor even influenced – by musicians or instrument makers, and certainly not by any 'folk' musicians. The state-political institutions that made these decisions did not have the slightest reason to encourage the production of accordions that can be played in Ireland. There was a Wall to prevent people from meeting and playing music together, so the compatibility of instruments for people playing traditional Irish music together was never an issue for decision-making in the GDR. These political reasons for keeping people apart have disappeared now, but the incompatible instruments are still there. Now, accordions are not exactly cheap instruments, and it is also difficult to get used to an instrument with a different technical layout. At the time they bought their instruments, GDR musicians did not have any choice. They could not travel to Ireland to buy differently tuned instruments. So they bought what was available in their local shops, and they played their repertoire in the keys that were available to them.

After the fall of the Wall, when musicians from East and West started to meet for sessions in Irish pubs, they discovered that their playing was incompatible because they were used to different keys. So the invisible Wall persisted for years, during which time former-GDR musicians had to replace their instruments and learn different playing techniques for traditional Irish music. Of course they had not *intentionally* transposed Irish tunes; they had had no choice of available keys on their instruments, and it may never have occurred to them that Irish tunes are played in specific keys that agree with all instruments normally used for this genre. Who should have taught them to hear tunes as being played in particular keys, and to imagine their own keys as incompatible in the hypothetical case of the Wall not being existent and themselves playing these tunes with other musicians in Ireland?

Fortunately accordions are not particularly dominant in Berlin Irish music sessions, and by 2016 former East and West musicians had widely learned how to coordinate their session playing. So we can say that there is a strong pressure observable in Berlin Irish session playing to conform to what can be described as formal (musicological) authenticity (cf. Taylor 1997). Musicians observe genre rules and playing techniques as perceived in the Irish home context, they aim at using the same keys for individual pieces, and indeed mostly instruments that are regarded as traditional for this genre. I say 'mostly' because, for instance, one girl occasionally brings along her German pipes and contributes an Irish tune or two on these, but the same thing happens in Belfast where one session player occasionally brings along his Bulgarian pipes for a short interlude. These contributions do not change the overall instrumentation of traditional Irish sessions, and neither do the Berlin musicians on the whole divert from traditional Irish repertoires. This is all the more astonishing because of the decidedly international composition of Berlin Irish session musicians.

What is different, though, concerns the occasional contribution of songs between the instrumental session performances. Whereas in Ireland there is a lot of respect for unaccompanied traditional singing and audience appreciation of its often free-rhythm beauty, German musicians with what are regarded for this genre as 'accompanying instruments' (such as guitar or bouzouki – see Chapter 1) seem to hear unaccompanied singing as 'incomplete' and tend to try to play along with the singing. However, this may also have something to do with the fact that many of the German Irish session musicians play in professional or semi-professional group formations who employ fixed arrangements for these songs when they play at community venues with stages or further afield.

National stereotyping about 'the Irish' held relatively little relevance for the musicians since they had been in musical communication across national boundaries for many years. Occasional articles in the local tabloids about 'a wild country, with wild music' and 'homesick Irish musicians in Berlin crying into their beer' were rejected unanimously by the local community musicians (cf. Schiller 2010). They were, however, indirectly affected because stereotypical images constructed in the media affect opinions of audience members who attend these Irish music community events. This was forcefully brought home to me when I attended a Berlin community concert in 2001, where I got into conversation with a slightly inebriated young man from *Lüneburg*, a town in northern Germany, who gave me this description of his views about 'Ireland' and 'the Irish':

> In Germany people live to work, and in Ireland people work to live. And if the Irish people wanted to take some time off work to just enjoy themselves then they would do just this. The Irish are thoroughly relaxed. They may work a bit to have some money, and then they will stop for a while to enjoy themselves, and then some time later they may decide to do another bit of work.

This young man worked in furniture fitting, and I asked him why he did not do just this in his own job. He replied that he felt restricted by his job, but that he would restrain himself to not live out this dream in Germany. But he frequently goes to concerts of Irish music, and when hearing Irish music he dreams that in Ireland everything would be alright. So Irish community music fulfils an important role for this young man's mental world, and such paradisiacal image constructions of audience members will also – possibly indirectly – feed back to the musicians. Again Ireland becomes the eternal 'otherworld' where everything is possible.

Not surprisingly, such image constructions do also affect local marketing strategies for CDs of these community musicians. Berlin resident Irish musician John Shanahan and his wife and musical partner, Regina Tichel, have been toying with the idea of establishing an indie recording label in Berlin, and they gave me some explanations about how cover images work with local audiences. According to John, if it says 'recorded in Berlin' on the cover, audiences think that it is 'low quality pub music'. If, on the other hand, it says 'recorded live in pubs in Ireland' it is not seen as 'low-quality' music. Consequently, whether these images hold any truth or not, local musicians are affected and will have to work with them.

So how do local musicians present their music to their audiences? Let us have a look at a few examples. The liner notes on Dave Bradfield's CD *Celtic Pulse* (see Figure 5.5) present the internationally mixed group of musicians to audiences as a 'group of friends'. The cover shows a photo of Dave playing his pipes in front of a drawing of a pub session. The liner notes (1995) say: 'I came to Berlin nearly 14 years ago and have fairly settled into a life away from Ireland but I have not forgotten my roots. I took up the pipes since I came over here and have been travelling every year for about 6 weeks to Clare, Galway, West Cork and Dublin learning and picking up tunes … This recording is a sample of some of what myself and a few friends play. We play mostly at parties and sessions.' The CD certainly has a flavour of what to me represents 'authentic' Berlin culture. Musicians like Dave and his friends will sell a few of these CDs to audience members who come along when they play somewhere in the community. And they will give away quite a few more. The CD will probably not sell well because it ignores the dictates of existing market categories, but that certainly does not make it poor music. Existing marketing categories may determine what makes music 'valuable' for sale, but musicians decide its quality. And they may choose to reflect the real roots of Irish music in Berlin. Sadly, however, many community venues closed in the 1990s as a result of the steeply rising rents after the fall of the Wall. By the late 1990s Dave's income from community performances had dwindled to such an extent that even in combination with income from his music shop and associated community projects, Dave was no longer able to support his family, forcing them to pack up and move to Italy, where earning an income from the combination of *Shiatsu* massage and community music-making was still possible.

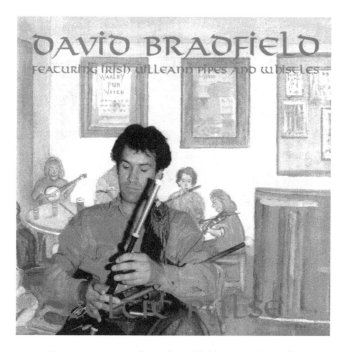

Figure 5.5. Cover of David Bradfield's CD *Celtic Pulse*

Eddie Smyth and Marty Byrne's CD *The Toetapper* (see Figure 5.6) uses different marketing strategies; it does not mention Berlin at all. Eddie and Marty go touring internationally, and they want to sell Irish music, not Irish music made in Berlin. In the liner notes *The Toetapper* is pretty delocalised, although it mentions 'learning pieces from Irish musicians', but also from other 'folk' musicians worldwide. The CD could have been made anywhere in Ireland, but also elsewhere, and that is the image that comes across. It is not dated either, so it is sort of free-flowing in space and time, thereby hinting at the 'timeless times' and 'boundless regions' of the elusive Celt, without actually slotting their music into the 'Celtic bin'. Musically it contains a mix of traditional Irish tunes and folk songs from different places, none of which refer to Berlin.

Figure 5.6. Cover of Eddie Smyth and Marty Byrne's CD *The Toetapper*

The Work of the Weavers (see Figure 5.7) by *The Irish Weavers* (Robbie Doyle and Güno van Leyen), on the other hand, is very localised. It is recorded in 2000 in Berlin-*Kreuzberg*, and it is addressing local audiences, but sort of leaving the door open to anyone anywhere. The liner notes are very brief, but bilingual, and they bring the global to the local audiences: 'The Irish Weavers want you to know that this CD contains only the finest hand-woven music from two honest tradesmen whose musical travels take them to Ireland, Scotland, England, Australia, America and Canada … we are available for nearly every occasion (concerts, festivals, parties, weddings … and even funerals) … almost anytime, almost anyplace.'

The CD seems to be selling pub music, since the back cover shows the local Irish music pub, *The Shannon*, which is given as a contact address. So the musicians appear to be Berlin-based, but floating around internationally.

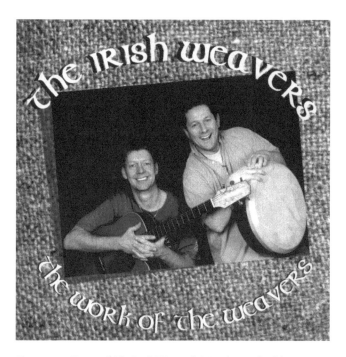

Figure 5.7. Cover of *The Irish Weavers'* CD *The Work of the Weavers*

There is very little traditional Irish dance music on this CD. It contains almost exclusively folk songs – some traditional, some new – and a lot of them deal with rambling Irishmen and alcoholic drink. So they are using these images to make the CD attractive to their audiences as well as to potential employers.

A different kettle of fish is the CD *Paddy on the Spree* (see Figure 5.8), produced by John Shanahan in 2003, featuring many members of the Berlin Irish music community as guest musicians: Regina Tichel, Inge Fiedler, 'Mac' Hugh McBrian, Detlef Skambraks, Max McColgan, Robbie Doyle, Bernd Lüdtke, Johnny Carr, Christian Tschirch, and Eddie Smyth, as well as a few contributors from outside the Berlin Irish community. The main musicians are John Shanahan himself and Marty Byrne, both singers and guitarists.

The images on the cover of this CD are multi-layered and this already shows in the title, *Paddy on the Spree*. The Spree is the main river running through Berlin, and this meaning is alluded to by the cover image showing

Figure 5.8. Cover of John Shanahan and Marty Byrne's CD *Paddy on the Spree*

the musicians standing (decidedly not 'dancing') beside a river, most likely the Spree. But since the CD is addressed mostly to local audiences, the meaning of the English language expression 'on the spree' is indicated (in a quotation from the *Oxford Dictionary*) inside the cover. So John and Regina have chosen a symbolic representation with a double meaning; one of these holding a specific meaning for local Berlin audiences, the other holding a general meaning for everyone else, and an additional meaning for anyone knowing the musicians to be from Berlin. The liner notes indicate that the CD was recorded in Berlin, but despite the stereotypical component of the 'lively or boisterous frolic ... frequently accompanied by drinking' displayed through the meaning of its title, the CD conveys multiple meanings. It does not look like 'pub music', and it does not sound like 'pub music' either, since it contains multi-layered arrangements. So we can say that this CD uses multiple symbolism in its title to address different audiences.

We can summarise then that there exists a lively Irish music community in Berlin that gives home to a variety of pub sessions, where professional, semi-professional, and non-professional musicians meet who share a long-term dedicated interest in this musical genre. These musicians observe musicological genre rules as they apply within the home context of Ireland, but they create and add their own context-specific local meanings to Irish music merchandise and stage presentations, so as to bring their music closer to local audiences. Apart from David Bradfield's CD *Celtic Pulse*, none of these CDs make specific mention of the 'Celtic' in their liner notes, but they certainly use traditional material from regions that are at present regarded as 'Celtic'. In this way the musicians avoid being slotted into a category of 'Celtic music', but they keep their options open how their CDs can be sold in musical outlets.

Also mentioned in this context of local Berlin Irish music merchandise should be Sandy Cheyne, who holds a special place within the Berlin Irish community. Originally from Aberdeen/Scotland, Sandy came to Berlin in 1982, when he was offered a post at the *Havel-School* to teach art to the children of British servicemen. When his work came to an end with the fall of the Wall, Sandy stayed on in Berlin, working as an artist. In the early 1990s Sandy visited many of the Irish music pubs and community sessions, as – according to his self-description – he 'likes Celtic music very much' (Cheyne 1994:3), and during this time he made drawings of many of the Irish community musicians in Berlin.

When Sandy met with the Irish fiddle player Francis Sim, they decided on the self-publication of a booklet (64 pages) featuring Sandy's drawings (see examples in Figure 5.9) in combination with transcriptions of traditional Irish and Scottish tunes by Francis. The booklet does not contain any other text apart from the short introduction of how it came into being. According to Sandy, the first edition consisted of eighty copies, and a second edition gives the number of forty copies. Francis, who is an instrument maker, has since moved to northern Germany, and Sandy, who – besides drawing – plays the banjo, has returned to Scotland. So it is highly unlikely that another edition of their booklet, *Die Irische Kneipenszene in Berlin* (1994), will come into existence, but Sandy's work is cherished within the Berlin Irish music scene and his drawings are passed around among the community musicians.

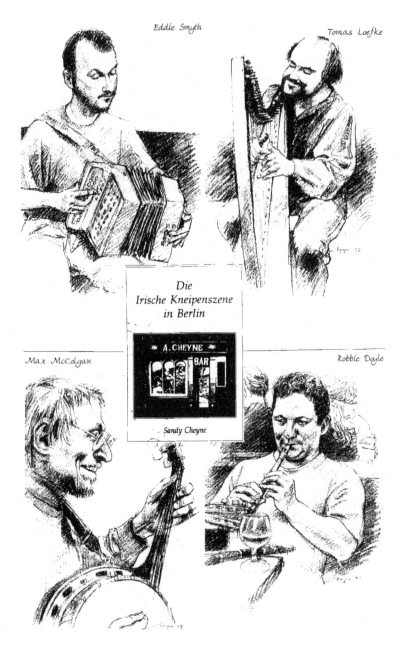

Figure 5.9. Examples of Sandy Cheyne's drawings of Berlin community musicians

When looking at how Irish music is reflected in the German media, it is most interesting to note that although traditional Irish music has been quite popular in Germany since the 1970s, it seems pretty much absent from programmes on national radio stations, and notable exceptions are regional and private radio stations. *Radio Multikulti*, which broadcast on FM in the wider Berlin region from 1994 to 2008, addressed foreign residents and Germans interested in music and culture from abroad, and featured contributions from all available international sources, including alternative-culture German songs, and traditional Irish music. Through voluntary involvement of its former employees it continued from 2008 as a private Internet radio station, which successfully led to a six-hour daily broadcast on FM again since 2010 on a non-commercial frequency.

As far as folk music repertoires are concerned, there was for a while a weekly programme, *Folkzeit*, on the local Berlin radio station *RadioBERLIN88,8*,[3] presented by Arno Clauss (himself a musician), which included traditional Irish music and a fair percentage of local Berlin folk musicians. The station does, however, continue to feature Irish music, live from Berlin venues, on St. Patrick's Day; therefore a certain representation of Irish music remains. So between them, these two sources for providing traditional Irish music on German radio have effectively established a musical link between the local and the global. And despite their quite different approaches, both these sources provided means to challenge dominant musical culture as presented in the German media (cf. Langlois 1996:260 on strategies to empower regional and minority interests in North African *Rai*).

Irish Music in Prague

The first time I travelled to Prague for research about Irish music was in 2007; therefore my research relates clearly to the post-socialist era. Although Prague always had a reputation for international openness, even during its

3   Also broadcasting online at www.radioberlin.de

communist period, since the Velvet Revolution of 1989 the international face of Prague has changed considerably. As in other post-socialist European countries, the opening of the first Irish pubs falls into the 1990s, and as far as I heard in response to my inquiries, the first one was the *James Joyce*, which sadly was destroyed in the flood of 2002. The follow-up Irish pub was the *Molly Malone's*, located in the northern part of the *Staré Město* (Old Town) district, which in 2010 changed its name back to *James Joyce*. It is pleasantly located in a small dead-end lane, which allows for indoor and outdoor seating. Much of its background music is related to traditional repertoires, but live music takes place mostly around St Patrick's Day. As the layout of the pub is very accommodating to session playing I asked the manager, Tony, if they ever held any traditional Irish session events. His answer sounded very confusing: 'No, we have tried, but session musicians took frequent breaks between their pieces, and this was chasing away customers.' No further information was coming forward. Why, I asked myself, should their customers run away if they are not continuously exposed to music?

There are a few other Irish bars in the city centre, such as *Rocky O'Reilly's* (a bar & restaurant), *J.J. Murphy's* (a sports bar, with GAA connections), or *Martin's Irish Pub* (advertised as a local for Czech speakers who like Irish food and drink), and in the north of the city the *Irish Club*, a B&B with a small bar attached. The *Irish Club* with its small beer garden was located in a leafy residential part of Prague, and it was not displaying the ubiquitous Guinness flags for decoration but unobtrusive bunting in the national colours of Ireland (see Plate 1). So I asked around in all these venues about their views on Irish live music. As I found out, none of these venues have any live music except for St. Patrick's Day special events.[4] When I asked why they were not interested in holding any traditional sessions, which would provide them with live music for no more expenses than a few complimentary drinks for the musicians, some of them told me that 'Czech Irish musicians were rather poor musicians'. As I found out later, this was another red herring to explain the non-existence of traditional Irish session playing in the city centre.

4   The *Irish Club* staff said they had tried live music for their guests, but that local residents in their quiet street had complained about it. Unfortunately in November 2016 the *Irish Club* closed its doors altogether.

When in 2007 a new Irish pub with live music interests opened in an arcade off Wenceslas Square, about five minutes' walk from *Hlavní Nádraži* (Prague's central train station), I paid it a visit to find out what was on offer on their stage. However, although they chose the traditional name *Shamrock* for their pub, they saw traditional Irish music – even in all its modern variants – as a 'special interest category' that is in performance best mixed with other repertoires, and as their resident musicians told me, this was indeed what was expected of them. The resident musicians in July and August 2007 were offering an eclectic mix of English and American folk-related pop-songs, interlaced with sets of traditional Irish tunes, some of which contained jazzy improvisational sections. The fiddle player with this outfit, Ondra Riegl, was a music student with an interest in jazz music, who on other occasions played with an Irish band.[5] Ondra related to me that he was introduced to Irish music by Eoghan O'Reilly, an Irish button accordion player who had settled in his home town of Šumperk – situated in the east of the Czech Republic – and that they had joined up with guitarist Radomir Flek to play Irish music in a group named *Bottlewash*. Much like the patterns I had found in Berlin, this showed the strong cultural influences of migrant Irish musicians who settle at a particular location and establish relations with local musicians. However, Ondra thought that there were no traditional Irish sessions taking place in Prague.

By 2012 the *Shamrock* had disappeared from the Prague Irish scene, but a *Dubliner* pub had opened up in *Staré Město*, and also *Caffrey's Irish Bar*, the latter with live music on several nights per week, some of it Irish music. For their 'Irish night' the pub featured the Czech band *The Beerberries*, a group of five music students and one member which they described as 'from a musical family'. Only one of the musicians spoke English, and he told me that they got their material from the Internet. Their repertoire consisted of some Irish and English folk songs, a few sea shanties, traditional Irish instrumental material, and an accordion Balkan tune that they said they had learnt from the playing of the Irish group *Solas*.

5   For a listening experience of Ondra's personal-style fusion of traditional Irish music and jazz go to https://www.youtube.com/watch?v=WpeFurcBllw. Other recordings that Ondra has since then uploaded to YouTube feature also a more traditional Irish orientation.

When I returned to *Caffrey's Irish Bar* in 2015, their management and bar staff *vociferously* denied that they had *ever* had this or any other band playing Irish music in their pub. I found this statement rather odd. Why this denial? After all, I had recorded some of this band's performance in 2012 in *Caffrey's Irish Bar*, and *The Beerberries* are undoubtedly skilled musicians. To solve this riddle, I had to extend my research to districts outside the city centre of Prague, and as it turned out, this now as 'non-existent' declared previous performance of *The Beerberries* was not the only Irish live music to be found in Prague. Indeed there exists a whole separate scene of 'special interest' musicians who meet annually for an Irish music Summer School (see Figures 5.10 and 5.11). A valuable source of information for locating this annual event – which surprisingly was not advertised in any of the Prague Irish pubs – was a hint that Ondra Riegl dropped in one of our conversations about Irish music.

Researching further into this topic, I found out that the Summer School had emerged in the post-*Riverdance* cultural climate, and it started off as a dance workshop in 2001 – with around 35 participants – organised by a group calling itself *Rinceoirí – Irish Dance Club* (first registered in 1997). According to information from one of its main organisers, Václav Bernard, the Summer School also draws international audiences – mainly from Poland, Slovakia, and Germany, but also some participants from Belgium, Norway, and Canada. Their main interest is still Irish dancing (all different styles), but over the years they have added instrumental workshops (fiddle, flute, whistle, bodhrán, guitar, uilleann pipes, concertina, and harp) and sean-nós singing, and since 2007 they have also offered an Irish language class relating to their taught Irish song material (such as the meaning of songs like *Bean Phaidín* and *Siúil a Rún*).

By 2016 the number of participants had risen into the hundreds, many of them returning every year. Some of the Summer School teachers are from the Czech Republic, others are brought in from Ireland for specific classes. Bernard's Summer School runs for a week in August, and on the last night there is a public performance of all participants, teachers and students, musicians and dancers, at a local theatre venue (see Plate 3).

Figure 5.10. Bodhrán class at Bernard's Summer School, Prague, with teacher Roman Kozák on right row at back

Figure 5.11. Irish pub session with 'Celtic' (Breton) dancing as part of Bernard's Summer School, Prague

During the week, Bernard's Summer School offers a variety of cultural events to the participants, such as film showings, an 'Irish quiz' night, or a ceili dance evening; in 2014 they held a public 'riverdance' event on the shores of the Vltava. And as I found out from bodhrán teacher Roman Kozák and flute teacher Radvan Markus, they also always organise a few session events in local pubs where students and teachers can get together to practise their newly learnt material as well as established old tunes. These venues are decidedly *not* Irish pubs, and they have no recorded music playing continuously in the background. It is here that the reason emerged why Irish session musicians in Prague have fallen out with all the Irish bars in the city centre: it was a lack of cultural understanding about the nature of traditional Irish sessions, as these are not stage events with fixed repertoires, and they fulfil an important role for musicians to exchange background information about their musical choices. So during an average session event natural breaks will emerge for verbal exchanges to take place. It is these that had led to quarrels with publicans in the city centre Irish pubs, because at these venues background music was switched on every time when musicians took a short break to exchange information about an item in their repertoire. To the musicians this was annoying because it interfered with their communication, and to the bar personnel it sounded like interruptions of their 'music programme', which might lose them customers. Because of these different expectations, Irish pubs in Prague have turned out incompatible with traditional music sessions. Apparently these different conceptualisations have led to a permanent split between Irish city centre bars in Prague and musicians who are seriously interested in traditional Irish music. The latter have taken to organising their own session events on an ad-hoc basis, and they avoid all contact with the city centre Irish bars. They do not even advertise their CDs in the city centre Irish venues, and neither does Bernard's Summer School find any display or mention there.

If we cast a comparative look back at the Irish session scene in Berlin, we can observe that here also a differentiation took place between Irish pubs in the city centre and *Irische Kneipen* in local community settings where regular session events took place. However, such a regularity to sessions was totally absent in Prague – and indeed within the wider context of the Czech Republic. In further conversations with teachers at Bernard's

Summer School I found out that more or less all Czech Irish session playing is organised on such a spontaneous basis, negotiated and coordinated by the interested musicians when and where a desire for session playing arises. Concertina teacher Tomáš Pergler told me about sessions in *Zach's Pub* in Pilsen and in the Smíchov area of Prague that are organised on such a flexible basis.[6] Another session, in the Scottish *Whisky and Kilt* pub (see Figure 5.12) in Prague, takes place monthly, but on different days of the week, as required for availability of the musicians, which is discussed and arranged via email or phone before setting the date with the publican, Vaçek. The pub has only two large tables and a few barstools along the bar; so with a dozen or more musicians in attendance there is not much space left for audiences, and the monthly event is indeed not much advertised except among musicians and their friends. So these are clearly not events to draw customers into bars, but communication events for local musicians.

Figure 5.12. Irish session at the *Whisky and Kilt* pub in Prague

6   For an audio-visual impression of members of the group *Poitín* playing in the Pilsen session go to https://www.youtube.com/watch?v=yz_HIJ6CjoM

The attraction of such sessions for musicians was confirmed when I asked some Summer School teachers and students specifically whether they preferred to play in sessions or at stage events. The majority of them stated that they preferred sessions, some said they liked both, but no one voiced a preference for stage playing. It should be pointed out here that all these musicians perform with professional or semi-professional bands, and most of them play a variety of other genres as well, such as classical music, jazz, bluegrass, or 'world music'. It would seem then that these musicians feel the same affinity for personal freedom to improvise and create spontaneously in informal session playing as Ioannis Tsioulakis (2011a, 2011b, 2021) describes in relation to jazz musicians in Athens, who distinguish in their music-making between 'work' and 'play'.

What these pubs have in common that are accepted by the musicians for session playing is that they respect the musicians and the cultural arrangements for session playing by not imposing background music during live music breaks. A new experimental project emerged in 2017 in a pub called *Beckett's* with newly refurbished garden seating. It is located in the centre of Prague, however not in the area much frequented by tourists, but rather in a local working class district. The publican, Zac, has an interest in traditional Irish music, and therefore he engages local Czech Irish bands like *Glíondar* or the *Jolly Buskers* for weekly live performances. For the celebration of their new garden he had arranged an outdoor traditional Irish session, which was much enjoyed by the local Czech audience. There was spontaneous applause for many sets, and a little girl of maybe two years of age started dancing enthusiastically to the music. So it seems that, at least in this part of Prague, traditional Irish music is welcomed in the community. It is to be hoped that the project will survive, especially since it has the support of local Irish musicians.

So how do these Czech musicians market their CDs, which they do not advertise in local Irish pubs? *Poitín* (with whom Tomáš Pergler plays) consists of five Czech musicians and an English singer/guitarist who is also a songwriter. Their CD *Wish* (2014) (see Figure 5.13) contains a mix of songs and sets of tunes, stylistically geared towards traditional Irish music. The outside cover is a nondescript grey landscape, which on the inside of the cover infuses with shades of pink. Ireland? Czech Republic? Dawn of

Figure 5.13. Cover of *Poitín*'s CD *Wish*

'timeless times' and 'boundless regions'? The cover gives no further clues, so listeners are challenged to construct their own images through the music. Their second CD, *Simple Pleasures* (2016) has a black-and-white photo of a Czech Irish pub session as its cover: a straightforward meaning to indicate its traditional musical contents.

Dún an Doras (with whom Radvan Markus plays) have a completely different approach. Their first CD, *Bossa Nudski* (1999) (see Figure 5.14), released by *Mars Records*, contains predominantly Irish traditional material, complemented by a few of their own compositions and some genre mixing, such as the *Macedonian Set*, which combines Balkan and Irish traditional music. *Sweet & Sour* (2003) and *Rua* (2005) were released on the Brno-based indie label *Indies Records*, and are stylistically a little more of a mixed bag: most of the music is closer to 'folk' than to 'traditional Irish', including more world music elements and some of their own compositions. The group came together in 1997 in Prague, and over the years has included a variety

Figure 5.14. Cover of *Dún an Doras*'s CD *Bossa Nudski*

of international musicians on diverse world music instruments, including 'traditional Irish' ones. *Dún an Doras* have on occasion been described as a 'Celtic folk-rock band', but their interests lie closer to 'world music' than to the 'Celtic' idiom. However, *Sweet & Sour* has an abstract image of red stripes on blue ground as its cover, and *Rua* has an abstract red-on-yellow cover image, making them both flexible to fit into different bins in record shops, including the 'Celtic' one. The cover of *Bossa Nudski* shows a red sandal on reddish ground, and some vague footprints at the back: stylised references to Irish dancing, which are continued on the inside of the cover.

The CD *Straight From the Bottle* (2006) (see Figure 5.15) by the *Bottlewash Band* (in which Ondra Riegl plays) again displays a rather different concept. The front cover is a collage of bits of music-related images, and the back cover shows the three musicians with fiddle, accordion, and guitar. *Bottlewash* came together in the 1990s, when Eoghan O'Reilly, an Irish button accordion player who had settled in Ondra's home town of Šumperk – situated in the east of the Czech Republic – joined up with

Figure 5.15. Cover of the *Bottlewash Band* CD *Straight From the Bottle*

guitarist Radomir Flek. As much as the musicians are a coming-together of Czech and Irish, so is the music on this CD. Traditional Irish, contemporary, and world music elements are mixed, and a number of songs are jointly written by Eoghan O'Reilly and Radek Flek. Self-produced mainly for promotional purposes at performance venues, it certainly does not neatly fit into the 'Celtic' slot. But since Irish music is marketed in the Czech Republic as 'World Music', such genre hybridity is welcomed by the existing market conditions; it allows the music to reach broader audiences and to blend well with Prague's image of being internationally open.[7]

7   A similar mixing of elements from different folk and traditional repertoires in performances seems to apply in St Petersburg, from where a colleague, David O'Kane, sent me some ethnographic recordings in 2006. Here, Irish music is also regarded as part of the category 'world music'.

So when we throw a comparative look at the Irish music scene in Berlin, where 'Irish Traditional' is sold as a separate category in record shops (i.e. not as 'World Music'), we can observe that far more mixing of genres, styles, and instrumentation takes place in the Czech Republic. However, this does not apply to Bernard's Summer School and its related sessions, which is exclusively focused on traditional genres, styles, and repertoires. Of course it cannot be denied that a thorough knowledge of traditional styles is a distinct advantage for a later mixing of styles, just as reading widely is advantageous for writers.

In conclusion we can therefore say that despite an observable lack of traditional Irish live music in the city centre of Prague, there is a lively interest in the Czech Republic of musicians to perform this genre, also within informal local session contexts. Locally created meanings of Irish music merchandise are more free-floating and flexible than in Berlin, but they are also less specific in communicating intended meanings. But one thing they have in common with the Irish music community in Berlin is that they also do not make use of any possibilities to market any historically based 'Celtic cousin' connections.

Not surprisingly, traditional Irish music does not feature on local radio in the Czech Republic, although there is a radio station dedicated to 'brass bands and folk music' played on acoustic instruments: *Radio Dechovka*.[8] However, they only broadcast Czech language songs (although not necessarily of Czech origin), and no instrumental music. Stylistically their programme includes folk, gospel, country music, and occasionally songs from pop music repertoires in folky arrangements. In this way their Czech language focus links the national with the international focus of repertoires.

Irish Music in Budapest

Before we continue our journey southward along the former Iron Curtain, let us briefly reflect that political borders in Europe have moved

---

8   Accessed FM in 2016, since 2009 they also broadcast as an online radio station, www.radiodechovka.cz

repeatedly over the last hundred years, and that an area that was once part of the Austro-Hungarian Empire has since then produced quite distinct national cultures with distinctly different concepts of 'Irish music'. With the possible exception of the two Germanys, this is maybe nowhere more strikingly apparent than between Austria and Hungary, and communist periods have certainly had a major influence on such divergence of image constructions.

A popular saying is quoted in the *Museum of Communism* in Prague, that the disintegration of communist power lasted in Poland for ten years, in Hungary for ten months, in East Germany for ten weeks, and in Czechoslovakia for ten days. However, cultural perceptions change slowly, and we have already seen in the description of Irish music in Berlin that some differences still exist over thirty years after the disappearance of the Wall.

My first interest in the Budapest Irish music scene was guided by a popular book classified in UK bookshops as 'non-fiction travel literature' (McCarthy 2000), in which a *McCarthy's* Irish pub is described as being located in Budapest and featuring live Irish music on stage, at least at St. Patrick's Day celebrations. As no 'McCarthy's Bar' existed in the local phone book, people at the hotel reception volunteered to help me by making some further inquiries, while I decided to take a look at the *Irish Cat Pub* that I had seen advertised locally. This place turned out a narrow L-shaped 'Irish Steak House' selling Irish food and drink to the locals, with no interest whatsoever in live music. In fact they gave me quite surprised looks that I was interested in Irish music. For live music I was referred to a pub at the far end of the city centre, named *Beckett's Ír Bár & Étterem* (Irish Bar and restaurant) (see Figure 5.16). When in that part of the town I came across a tourist guide I asked her for directions. She sounded not particularly enamoured by my question and replied in a way that sounded rather antagonistic to visitors, 'You come here, and then you eat and drink your own.' I found my way to the *Beckett's* nevertheless, but had gained the impression that her response indicated ethnic, rather than European identity constructions.

The *Beckett's* is a rather spacious venue, and it offers Hungarian, Irish and other food, as well as Irish and other drink, they have lots of screens for watching sports events, and they have a stage on which at weekends (Friday, Saturday, and Sunday) bands play very loud – mostly American – pop

Figure 5.16. *Beckett's Ír Bár & Étterem* (Irish Bar & Restaurant) in Budapest

music and occasionally some jazz/blues. I tried to elicit some information from the bar staff how they felt about Irish music in an Irish venue,
to which they expressly stated that they *never* had any Irish live music, as
this was regarded as a rather quaint minority interest. Surely Irish music
could not sound *that* quaint to Hungarians when it was hugely popular
just 150 miles further west in Vienna? Sadly no other information was
forthcoming in this venue.

From whatever live music I perceived on offer at other locations in
the city (reggae, jazz, Latin disco music) it seems that Irish music does
not fit well with the progressive Western image that many locals wish to
present. Even their own folk music seems to have disappeared into highly

formal stage shows specifically aimed at particular tourist tastes, and 'Gypsy music' – internationally widely associated with Hungarian culture – seems also to be affected by this trend of 'Westernisation'. According to the weekly English language paper, *The Budapest Times*,[9] Gypsy music had disappeared recently from *Hungarian Radio* as part of a reorganisation process, and fewer venues offer employment now to Gypsy bands.

In the introduction to a detailed anthropological study of post-socialist changes in eastern Europe, Maruška Svašek (2006:20–1) has drawn attention to recent racist discrimination against Gypsies at various eastern European locations (some post-socialist settings involving Hungarians, Russians, Serbs, and Czechs). And although in some contexts Gypsy music was seen as 'a true repository for expressing socio-cultural hurt and suffering' (van de Port 1998), it seems that at least in Budapest this image does not sit well with the widely desired image of modernisation and Westernisation. Neither does Irish music, apparently, which may have something to do with negative memories of state-controlled versions of folk music in their recent past.

Looking at Balkan images of 'Gypsy music', Carol Silverman (2007:339) points out that during the socialist period government regulations in Romania and Bulgaria had prohibited Roma from playing their music in public and from travelling abroad, but that in the 1990s widespread Western European interests emerged for 'Gypsy music' in Balkan countries. She also observes that within this context gypsies are often seen as 'keepers of something pure, traditional, that is lost elsewhere'. Silverman found that, rather than contesting this stereotype, gypsies tended to use it for their own benefit. This may well be their best choice because, as Edward Said (2005) observed, stereotypes as presented by the mass media do not change. Said thought that interest groups and academics may change views among their community, but that the mass media would continue their presentations. So it seems that gypsies are indeed best off by exploiting these stereotypical images for their own benefit. After all, this is the same strategy that some Irish immigrants employed for the stage in nineteenth-century America when confronted by national stereotyping (Williams 1996).

9   *The Budapest Times*, 30 July to 5 August 2007

But to return to the Budapest context: anything 'folksy' appeared to be seen as backward looking, and the same conditions applied to Budapest's Scottish Pub & Restaurant, *The Caledonia*, which likewise concentrates on gastronomic culture and transmission of sports events. It seems that although post-socialist culture in Budapest is open to cultural influences from Western Europe, this does not include an interest in their folk music cultures. This is all the more remarkable since these pubs came into existence in the post-socialist period, at a time when the export of Irish pub session culture has reached far and wide, for instance to quite distant places like Hong Kong, Lhasa, and Thailand (Wilkinson 1999:284). Admittedly most of these cater predominantly for local expatriate communities, but quite frequently they offer traditional Irish music on a regular basis.

As I found out during my research, the *Beckett's* has been in existence since 1994, prides itself on being knowledgeable about the local Irish scene, and none of their staff had ever heard of a place called *McCarthy's*. Neither did the helpful receptionists at the hotel discover any trace of such a place. Maybe the Guinness served at the said *McCarthy's* on St. Patrick's Day was so strong that the author of *McCarthy's Bar* (2000) forgot in which city he had actually been, for it appears to not have been Budapest. But then: why let the truth get in the way of a good story ...

According to personal information in 2008 from Hungarian scholar, Eglantina Remport, at the time a PhD student at Queen's University Belfast, there is a 'private interest' scene of Irish music in Budapest, but unfortunately it turned out so private that even she was not able to establish any research contact: nobody wanted to be interviewed about Irish music. It may well be that this tendency to secrecy is a leftover from the communist period, and as such I think it is best left undisturbed until people feel confident to talk about it.

We can conclude then that in the early twenty-first century there is no public traditional Irish music scene observable in Budapest. If the Hungarian capital is still mentally closed to integrating Irish music in local Irish bars, it seems highly unlikely that it may exist anywhere else in Hungary, and therefore questions about Irish session culture and 'Celtic cousin' aspirations do not arise at all. It is highly relevant, though, that such strong negative images about Irish music are so widely encountered in a major city in Hungary, less than 150 miles distant from Vienna. It explains to a certain extent why local musicians interested in Irish music may not have been keen to have been interviewed.

Irish Music in Bucharest

Bucharest presents a rather similar face to the Budapest context as regards Irish music. According to *Bucharest in Your Pocket* (April-May 2012), the *Dubliner* was the first Irish pub to open in Bucharest in 1995. It offers some Irish food and drink, and a wide range of sports (courtesy of Sky TV), but their staff declared that they 'never have any live Irish music'. Apparently the only Irish pub in Bucharest that has any live music at all is *O'Hara's Irish Pub* (see Figure 5.17) in *Strada Franceză*, in the Old Town centre, near Bucharest University. Their staff told me that for a while they had a singer/guitarist for an Irish music night on Thursdays, but that this

Figure 5.17. *O'Hara's Irish Pub* in Bucharest

was not the case any longer, and they certainly never had any traditional Irish sessions.

There are a few 'Irish pubs' in the Old Town centre, but they are only so by name. None of them displayed any cultural decorations relating to Ireland. These Old Town centre pubs mostly consist of outdoor seating to accommodate tourists, and they are more or less all in a standard format. The 'Irish pub' beer garden will be decorated with little *Guinness* flags, the 'Czech pub' beer garden will be decorated with little *Staropramen* flags and similar brewery advertisements. Snippets of American style pop music waft through the Old Town centre, and with a bit of luck one might encounter a 'gypsy style' fiddler, employed by one of the many pubs to play outside their venue in the street to attract tourists into the pub.

So we can observe that in Bucharest music is not used as an identity marker for any particular nationalities (apart from the stereotypical 'Balkan Gypsy music'), and that there is also no observable traditional Irish music scene to be found in Bucharest. It is quite possible that this has similar 'tendency-to-secrecy' associations as in Budapest, but as far as the public face is concerned, it points to the conclusion that no Irish session culture and no 'Celtic cousin' aspirations exist in Bucharest either. Given the presently growing worldwide popularity of Irish session playing, it is certainly an interesting research finding that no such indications exist in Bucharest. This suggests that the view expressed in Barta (2013) still very much applies here that the newly post-socialist European countries are still searching for their identities. It may also have something to do with a lack of expatriate musicians having settled in Bucharest because, as we have already seen within other European contexts, it is frequently the inspiration of locally resident Irish musicians that gets an interest in Irish session playing established. Community sessions usually start around Irish musicians who attract local musicians with an interest in learning to play Irish music. It is at these community musical exchanges that extra-musical information is passed on, and thereby they become an outpost of the Irish musical tradition. In this way they can serve as a good indicator for how Irish music and 'the Celtic' are conceptualised within their respective wider cultural contexts.

This does not mean, of course, that there are no individual musicians in the Balkan area who are inspired by Irish musical material. For instance, *The*

Orthodox Celts from Belgrade, Serbia, have been giving stage performances at various Balkan area locations since 1992. They are a seven-piece folk-rock band, influenced, among others, by *The Pogues*, and using Serbian bagpipes besides Irish traditional instruments in their stage performances. But their repertoire is mostly song-based, and they are highly unlikely to drop into local Irish bars to start a community Irish session tradition. Their interest is rather aligned to current rock and pop music trends and focused on stage performances. There is at present no cultural incentive in place for them to motivate their audiences to pick up community Irish session playing.

So for our inquiry we can extract here no further information because stage events work to a different dynamic, may mix musical genres and styles every which way, and lack grassroots connections with local community music-making events. Since our interest is in finding out how Irish cultural concepts transfer to other locations in Europe, our focus needs to remain on Irish community activities where cultural concepts of the Irish musical tradition are passed on between musicians, with a view to cultural intimacy.

Irish Music in Vienna

Although my first visit to Vienna in 2007 was comparatively rather short, it was nevertheless highly impressive. So many historical and cultural developments have linked Austria with Hungary, as well as with Prague and indeed with Germany, that a visit to Vienna suggested itself as an essential addition to this comparative study. The train journey from Bratislava (Slovakia) to Vienna (Austria) takes around twenty minutes, but during this short journey it becomes amazingly obvious that we have crossed a cultural borderline.

After having spent a month with musical research in the Czech Republic and Hungary, the most striking and immediate impression on arriving in Vienna came from its musical street culture: music was everywhere, out in the open, offering a truly multicultural face and accommodating all levels of confidence, be it music students practising their guitars, or professional singers offering some opera/operetta on a city centre street corner. After the sparse cultural fare of the occasional 'gypsy fiddler' in Bucharest, the 'traditional jazz band' playing their standard set of music every day on Prague's Charles Bridge, and the total lack of any street music in Budapest, I perceived the multicultural offers in Vienna as almost overwhelming, and in the pedestrian area of the *Kärntnerstraße* they certainly exuded a feeling of exuberance.

Not surprisingly, there are also a variety of Irish pubs in Vienna, and they cater for distinctly different audiences. The *Shamrock Pub*, for instance, is a sort of hip-hop place – with two big screens for watching sports – that caters for people who like Irish beer, while the *Flanagan* has more traditional tastes. The latter have imported their complete traditional-style bar in the 1990s from a pub in Churchtown, County Cork, and had it reassembled in Vienna by Irish craftsmen. They advertise as a sports bar, with plenty of screens for their customers, but they use Irish background music regularly, and on special occasions – like St. Patrick's Day – they engage musicians to provide Irish live music for their customers. Staff at the *Flanagan* told me about the *Pickwick's*, a bar-cum-English language bookshop where regular Irish sessions took place (see Figure 5.18). During the summer these were monthly sessions, but at other times they were more likely to take place weekly.

The session I was lucky to participate in during the summer of 2007 was attended by a mixture of local Austrian and Irish musicians. Their instrumentation agreed with what is presently regarded as traditional for this genre, and the repertoire was certainly Irish, although it contained a somewhat higher component of songs to instrumental pieces than the average home Irish session and many other sessions I attended during my research in Europe.[10] Sessions may not be addressed to audiences as such, but they nevertheless involve communication skills that require reading the audience to lead to an enjoyable event.

At this particular venue sessions are not so much motivated by staff desires to attract customers to the bar (in fact the bar closed early during the session event), but rather for serving as a cultural advertisement for the bookshop. The participating musicians enjoy having use of the facilities for

---

10   People at various European Irish session contexts have commented that interspersing sessions with songs makes them more palatable to European audiences, as instrumental pieces tend to sound to them 'all the same'.

Figure 5.18. Irish session at the *Pickwick Bookshop*, Vienna

getting together to play traditional Irish music. They told me that they make use of the Internet to organise sessions. Any planned sessions (also at other locations) are advertised on the *Tradivarium* website (www.tradivarium.at), which calls itself *Offene Plattform ... für Folk, Weltmusik und Verwandtes ... in Österreich*, advertising a flexible focus on folk and world music. It certainly offers a wide enough definition of its focus to include traditional Irish sessions. Also advertised on this website were sessions in a Scottish pub named *The Highlander*, which is situated near the main university of Vienna.

On a summertime visit in 2012 all the Irish session musicians appeared to be on a summer break, but when I returned to Vienna in 2017, the *Pickwick* sessions had ceased altogether. Likewise had those in the *Highlander*, and in a pub called *Backbone*, run by an Indian publican, which had had monthly Irish sessions for a while. However, there were two monthly sessions taking place in 2017: in the *Nâzim Hikmet Kultur Café* (see Figure 5.20) and in the *Café Concerto* (see Figure 5.21). Until the

Figure 5.19. Cover of the *Spinning Wheel* CD *The Maid on the Shore*

summer of 2017 there had also been a monthly session in the *Brandstetter*, which had been attended by some of the musicians that I met in the *Nâzim Hikmet Kultur Café*. The *Nâzim Hikmet* is a bar & café, accommodating different cultural events, one of which is the monthly Irish session. It is run by a publican from Ankara, and Turkish background music was playing before the start of the session. The musicians were mostly Austrian, with one Breton and a few Irish participants. During the event they gave me a CD that they had recorded with different musicians who had frequented this particular session over time, participating as guest musicians to the group *Spinning Wheel*.

The CD *The Maid on the Shore* (see Figure 5.19) contains Welsh, Breton, Irish, Scottish, and Galician material, and the theme of the cover hints at Celtic countries being perceived as close to seacoasts (the 'Celtic fringe' image). The CD cover quotes a description by Donna Bird as 'the band members having a great affinity for pan-Celtic music'. However, given Vienna's multicultural and world music interests, this seems rather a special focus within this broader vista of music than a tendency towards constructing a 'Celtic cousin' relationship.

Figure 5.20. Irish session at the *Nâzim Hikmet Kultur Café* and bar, Vienna

Figure 5.21. Irish session at the *Café Concerto*, Vienna

The *Café Concerto* is quite a different kettle of fish, although its background music before the session was also Turkish. The *Café Concerto* hosts diverse events, like songwriters nights; Folk, World, and Roots Music sessions; and the monthly Irish sessions. On the occasion when I attended, they held two different sessions on the same night: a jazz session downstairs and the Irish session upstairs. Two of the present musicians participated in both sessions consecutively. Both events were advertised on large notice boards outside the pub for the attention of interested customers, and both sessions were well attended, by musicians as well as by audiences. The repertoire at the Irish session consisted largely of common session material known to many musicians, as opposed to the more professionally flavoured *Nâzim Hikmet* session. Again the vast majority of attending musicians were Austrian, and a few of them told me that they were particularly attracted by the informality of the Irish session playing. Some of them were clearly early learners of Irish music, but there were also quite a few highly accomplished musicians present. So this session is well suited for communicating repertoires and playing styles for learners while passing on social customs of Irish session etiquette.

There are certainly also venues in Vienna where Irish music only occasionally makes an appearance, and sometimes these are even Irish pubs. Most beguiling among these I found an Irish pub called *Wind & Mill Pub*, owned by a man named Liu Zhong Wei and his son, and I was wondering what their interest might be in running an Irish pub in Vienna. As it turned out, their family had been living in Austria for many generations, and they had inherited the Irish pub. Their live music interests are equally multicultural: they do not cater for traditional Irish sessions, but they stage occasional jazz concerts, and at irregular times they have other live music. These events sometimes include Irish music, and on occasion the publican (senior) himself sings rap. This multicultural snapshot can maybe stand here as a vivid reflection of the adaptability of Vienna's Irish music scene: it seems to be capable to fit in with its diverse cultural surroundings, and it certainly does not aim at establishing any historical root connections with the *Hallstatt* culture to claim any 'Celtic cousin' connections. But then, given Austria's diverse and extensive European music connections, it would indeed be surprising to find any special attention directed towards establishing 'Celtic cousin' connections.

What becomes obvious, though, is that we find ourselves again within a cultural context where Irish session playing is appreciated. From what the session musicians at the *Pickwick* told me, it is during the autumn and winter season that traditional Irish sessions are plentiful. Some of Vienna's Irish musicians will then play at two sessions per week, and although overall different musicians go to different sessions, there is a certain amount of overlap. This arrangement fits in nicely with the Irish concept of meeting and exchanging musical information at sessions, but also with informally rehearsing material that the musicians can then use on other occasions for stage performances. If for the latter purpose extra sessions are needed the musicians will arrange them in advance among themselves and with the desired venue.

In conclusion we can then say that Irish session playing in Vienna is a little more flexible than in Berlin, but certainly a lot more regular than in Prague. Sessions are carried by cooperation between local Austrian and Irish musicians, they follow the traditional session procedures as practised in Ireland, and there are no observable attempts to establish any 'Celtic cousin' images on the basis of ancient cultures in Europe. Rather, there is a widely observable interest in a very broad vista of musical genres, with a partial overlap of musicians between genres. So Irish music in Vienna can best be described as a special interest within the wider field of world music. It is therefore not surprising that Irish session playing is not specifically associated with Irish pubs, but rather with 'cultural events' venues.

Irish Music in Istanbul

The first time I heard about the traditional Irish session in the *James Joyce* (see Figure 5.22) in Istanbul, was at an Irish session in Berlin in 2000, where a fiddle player related that she had participated in this session on her visit during the previous summer. Understandably I was immediately intrigued, but it was not until 2012 that I was able to travel to Istanbul. And yes, the session at the *James Joyce* was still going on, taking place on a weekly basis except for a break during the hottest summer months, when the local Irish musicians like to pay a visit home to Ireland. This is pretty good going for any regular traditional Irish session, and so Istanbul's *James Joyce* certainly deserved some closer ethnographic attention.

The *James Joyce* opened in 1996 as a hotel for Irish visitors to Istanbul, offering them the possibility to relax in their attached Irish pub. Local Belfast musician, Jason O'Rourke, told me that the *James Joyce* was originally located near *Taksim Square*, where he had visited it, but it has since moved to a small side street of *Istiklal Caddesi*, the main pedestrian walkway through *Beyoğlu*, the European area of Istanbul. Some of their staff are Turkish, some are Irish, and their pub is decorated with a multitude of small cultural artefacts, Irish and Turkish. At the back of the pub is a section with English language books, mostly by Irish authors, for free use of their guests/patrons, and their live music programme is mixed as well, including some 'Balkan folk music' and some American-flavoured popular musical fare, taking place on a small stage. Sunday night is Irish session night, and over the years it has seen participation of Irish and Turkish musicians as well as international visitors involved in Irish session playing.

The *James Joyce* session was initiated – and continues to be organised – by Irish fiddle player and proprietor of the *James Joyce*, Eamonn Lehane, with regular fellow musicians Jenny Miller (fiddle), Fergal O'Rourke (guitar, bouzouki), and Bob Beer (guitar, five-string banjo). Nilüfer Ketenci (fiddle, tambura-banjo) was also a regular at this session, but now has demanding responsibilities for the *Polka Café* in *Kadıköy*, an area on the Asian side of Istanbul which is much frequented by students, where she runs irregular Irish sessions and occasional other live music events. The *Kadıköy* Irish session (see Figure 5.23) also has a variety of international participants, often visiting musicians who are interested in Irish music. For instance, in 2015 French musician, Dominique Renaudin (button accordion), who was staying in Istanbul for a few months, regularly attended both sessions.

The *Kadıköy* session is a lot more flexible as regards integration of different musical genres. This can, of course, partly be explained by the fact that Nilüfer Ketenci and her fellow *Celteast* musician, Zeynel Sağ, play also Turkish and Balkan folk music besides their Irish repertoire, but varied contributions from visiting western musicians are equally welcome here.

Figure 5.22. Irish session at the *James Joyce Pub* in Istanbul-Beyoğlu

Figure 5.23. Nilüfer Ketenci and Zeynel Sağ at the Irish session in the *Polka Café* in Istanbul-Kadıköy

As regards the *James Joyce* session, it is interesting to observe that, although Bob Beer is interested in Turkish bağlama music, this type of music never enters the *James Joyce* sessions. In fact it is treated here very much as 'taboo' by the Irish musicians, despite American old-timey music easily being integrated into their session. The explanation that Eamonn Lehane gave for this was that their Turkish patrons expected a 'somewhat foreign' musical entertainment, however 'not too foreign'. Therefore Turkish folk and Arabesk influences were not agreeable for their live music offers.

A further interesting case is also the attitude of two teenage student Kurdish musicians, brothers Nezih and Kağan (small Balkan pipes/whistle and guitar/mandolin), who attended the *James Joyce* session for a while, but lacked all understanding for the concept of informal meetings with learning and sharing music in sessions. I heard it said from different sides that these two musicians are solely interested in repeating their fixed learnt repertoire at venues where payment is involved. They play occasionally in the *U2 Irish Pub*, a venue about the size of a large bath towel, also situated in *Beyoğlu*, but have given up all interest in session playing when it turned out to be a performance form that is not being paid for.

So we can observe that participants at these respective traditional Irish music events have quite different attitudes towards genre mixing, which for session playing is predominantly influenced by the musicians responsible for their organisation. The Irish/English/American dominated session group allows some contributions from other western folk genres. The Turkish based session in *Kadıköy* integrates contributions from eastern and western folk genres. And the two Kurdish students play a fixed, solely Irish repertoire on their own, without any session involvement.

And then there is Kate Fennell, 'Turkey Kate', who in 2013 had organised an exciting, colourful four-day 'Celtic Sounds Festival' in Istanbul,[11] courtesy of Culture Ireland and the Turkish Ministry of Culture and Tourism, with concerts, sessions, and Irish-Turkish cultural exchange music and dance workshops. Some Irish musicians had flown in for this event, and Black Sea musicians were expected to arrive on the following day,

11   Its full title was 'Celtic Sounds Irish Music and Culture Festival'. The workshops were intended to highlight the Galatian Celtic connection.

when on the very next morning the *Gezi Park* protests broke out. Over the weekend the street protests were met with water cannons and repeated tear gas attacks from the police. The original protests against plans to turn *Gezi Park* into a further *Beyoğlu* shopping mall were soon joined by an increasing crowd of protestors about the undermining of people's rights in recent years. A protest camp was set up in *Gezi Park*, and all surrounding streets and lanes in *Beyoğlu* were filled with cheering and shifting throngs of protestors waving flags of Kemal Atatürk, the founder of Turkey as a secular republic and nowadays a symbolic expression for people's right to self-determination.

When I went up to *Taksim Square* two days later to see how things were developing, the *Taksim Anıtı* – Monument of the Republic had been adorned with flags and protest paraphernalia (see Plates 4 and 5), while *Gezi Park* had been transformed into a protest camp of tents, and journalists from local radio and television stations were interviewing protestors. People from different backgrounds were mixing in their demand for human rights, and their hopeful joyful spirit was infectious. But nothing had prepared me for the emotional impact of hearing *Aziz Istanbul* (Beloved Istanbul) played from a parked van on *Taksim Square*. In *The Republic of Love* (2010) Martin Stokes describes how this song and its music address on various levels issues of nostalgia, changing cultural intimacy, and Istanbul's rapidly changing city scape. My knowledge of the Turkish language is rather basic, but I did not need too many translations to understand how deeply these people gathered at *Gezi Park* love their city. Maybe it was the context, maybe it was my mood, and maybe it was this quality of music that can express without words what no words can, but for the evening session at the *James Joyce* the mood and its message had spread to all the musicians present.

The *James Joyce* is at a distance of about ten minutes' walk from *Gezi Park/Taksim Square*, but fortunately it is in a small side street, and so it turned out to be the only venue where any festival-related music-making took place over this weekend. All other events had to be cancelled because none of the venues were accessible to audiences, and in any case everyone's interests were focused on these very different, political events. So, although we had some fantastic pub sessions in the *James Joyce* over the weekend, sadly most of the planned festival events did not take place at all. 'Turkey

Kate' has more recently returned to Ireland, and so any plans for Irish-Turkish cultural exchange festivals in the future are more likely to develop for taking place in Ireland instead. It is certainly sad that this promising idea never came to fruition in Istanbul in the summer of 2013.

Also sharing our hide-out of musicians sympathising with demands for people's rights during this weekend was music journalist, Paul O'Connor, who had also had high hopes for the *Celtic Sounds Festival*. Intending to write about musicians and musical exchanges, he ended up writing instead about a memorable popular protest in the streets of Istanbul against growing restrictions on people's rights in contemporary Turkey.

Fortunately I was able to return to Istanbul for visits in 2014 to 2019, to have another look at the community Irish music scene during slightly less turbulent times, and to elicit some more detailed information from the local musicians. When looking at their preferences between session playing and stage performances, the Turkish musicians expressed a clear preference for session settings and street music, although some of them also play in professional groups (mixed world music, western classical music). Among the *James Joyce* western musicians opinions were not so clear-cut: Jenny also participates in the local rock music scene, and additionally Jenny, Fergal, and Bob are members of an American old-timey folk group, the *Cupboard Creek String Band*. Nevertheless they are all strongly committed to their weekly Irish session in the *James Joyce*, and by 2019 Jenny had succeeded in interesting two members of her country band, Yann and Aaron, to participate in the *James Joyce* Irish session as well. Eamonn Lehane has even written a song about going in search of a session during a home visit to Ireland, which is included on the CD *Made in Istanbul* (see Figure 5.24) that he has recorded in 2011–12 with the Turkish musicians from the group *Celteast*.[12] The outside cover of this CD shows different images of the Bosphorus; the inside text is bilingual, makes mention of Galatian Celtic culture, and introduces all participating musicians individually. In addition, it shows a photo of the musicians at a session in the *James Joyce*, giving the pub as a contact address: a fine means to advertise 'Celtic cousin' cross-cultural musical cooperation.

12   For a listening experience of Eamonn Lehane's cooperation with *Celteast* go to https://www.youtube.com/watch?v=52ZzSES-K-Y and https://www.youtube.com/watch?v=406tIbnjSJE

Figure 5.24. Cover of Eamonn Lehane and *Celteast*'s CD *Made in Istanbul*

Also interesting about Turkish musicians playing traditional Irish music is that they are aware of what instruments are considered suitable in Ireland for playing this musical genre, but that they do not restrict themselves to these. Nilüfer Ketenci, for instance, employs her small Balkan-style banjo, the *tambura*, in equal measure as her fiddle for playing traditional Irish music. Zeynel Sağ, a student of western classical music and a fellow member of *Celteast*, plays a ukulele for this genre. And one of the teenage Kurdish brothers uses a *gaida*, a Turkish type of pipes, for Irish music. Since all these musicians employ genre-specific Irish phrasing and ornamentation, it is obvious that their choice of these instruments is intentional, that they regard them as suitable for this genre.

Another indication that this is not just accidental mixing of instruments because of a lack of 'traditional Irish instruments' is that the two percussionists who participated in sessions took care to bring along their

Irish bodhráns, playing them in traditional Irish style, and they never used any Turkish folk drums instead, which have indeed a very different timbre.

Turkish folk drums are used widely for street music in Istanbul, especially in the combination of *zurna* (a shawm, an oboe-type instrument of timbre and volume quite similar to that of the Breton *bombarde*) and *davul* (the traditional double-headed drum accompanying it). These instruments are commonly used to play music associated with the Black Sea region, to which any number of participants can join in to perform Black Sea line dances. Nowadays this genre is used widely for national identity expressions; it was employed in the *Gezi Park* protest camp during the 2013 confrontations, and during the elections of 2015 it was used by a variety of political parties as an expression of identity during public election events.

There are also frame drums in use for Turkish folk and Arabesk music, but their skins are considerably thinner than those used for bodhráns, and they are played by hand, not with any sticks, and so again their timbre is completely different from that required for an Irish session (for a detailed discussion about treatments of goat skins for different timbres and types of drums please refer to my description in Schiller 2001, especially pages 1–40). So in this regard it highlights a fine sensitivity to Irish music of those Turkish musicians who play Irish drums, and in an Irish style, for these sessions.

Therefore in conclusion we can say that we find a conscious, clear separation of musical genres and their associations where identity constructions are involved. On the other hand, Eamonn Lehane's CD with *Celteast* (2012) uses the title *Made in Istanbul*, an indication of cultural 'double-consciousness' – although not necessarily in Paul Gilroy's (1993) sense – and a nod towards 'common Celtic roots'. This makes Istanbul a rather unique cultural context for traditional Irish music, and as regards the focus of this publication it raises an interesting question: is the interpretation of Irish culture and traditional Irish pub sessions in Istanbul closer to the understanding of 'western' countries, or is it closer to cultural concepts of post-socialist eastern Europe? Its explorative attitude towards instrumentation certainly sets it apart from the community Irish music scene in Germany, Austria, and the Czech Republic. On the other hand its interest in displaying combinations of Turkish and Irish cultural paraphernalia in the *James Joyce*, as well as the historical interests at Ege University to explore common Celtic roots (see Chapter 6), indicate a rather different cultural interpretation from those contexts of the Hungarian and Romanian Irish bars described in this study.

Certainly of relevance to emerging image constructions and local cultural interpretations of Irish music in Istanbul will be the fact that it is 'too outlandish' to be of interest to the Turkish mass media, thereby leaving much leeway to individuals' creative interpretations of experiencing this musical genre within their local cultural context. Of course Istanbul is full of a most amazing mix of musical sounds, as for instance Fatih Akin's (2005) documentary film *Crossing the Bridge: The Sound of Istanbul* has fascinatingly illustrated: psychedelic underground music, rock, rap, breakdance, religious music, whirling dervishes, Kurdish ballads, Arabesk, Turkish classical music, street music of many different shades ... But then, Berlin certainly has a similarly diversified musical mix on offer, although their understanding of how to play traditional Irish sessions is culturally rather differently coloured.

I would not wish to contribute to national stereotyping by suggesting that the German musicians desire everything to be 'precise and correct', noting that the Czech musicians did the same, and especially since the multiplicity of genres in Fatih Akin's documentary (2005) is expressed and narrated by Berlin rock musician, Alexander Hacke. So it would seem that culture-specific interpretations of traditional Irish session performances – and associated Irish culture – are strongly coloured by images disseminated by the respective mass media interpretations, and the less there are of these influences, the more there will be of local creativity for interpretation. And just as Fatih Akin and Alexander Hacke see Istanbul's music scene as bridging Europe and Asia, so we may interpret the traditional Irish session music in Istanbul as integrating elements from east and west, resulting in a unique cultural combination, 'made in Istanbul'.

After all, musical interpretations are a response of diverse individuals to their cultural surroundings, and if they do not fit into imagined categories relating to academic theories then this indicates that the theoretical framework was conceptualised too narrow. There may be extra-musical as well as musical conventions for Irish session playing, but these are not cut out in black and white; they are at least in some regards flexible. Again it is Martin Stokes who has succinctly drawn our attention to this point:

> People can equally use music to locate themselves in quite idiosyncratic and plural ways … A moment's reflection of our own musical practices brings home to us the sheer profusion of identities and selves that we possess. (Stokes 1994:3–4)

Socio-cultural meanings of musical performances are malleable, created and changed within specific contexts, and – although this may go against the grain for 'purist' interpretations of traditional music *aficionados* in Ireland – musical meanings created by one group of people are not 'inherently better' than those created by another group of people. In his study of a visit of Black Sea musicians to Ireland in 1989, Stokes (1994:97–115) describes how meanings regarding regional identities and ascribed hierarchies changed over a week of musical encounters between the visiting Turkish and local Irish musicians during a range of small-scale musical events, including some pub sessions. The ethnographic detail contained in his study is a fitting reminder that the ethnographic descriptions in this present chapter relate also to specific times, locations, and encounters between specific musicians, and that they present only a slice of how traditional Irish music is perceived and interpreted at these different European locations.

Conclusion

In this chapter we have observed that there are certain commonalities between 'western capitalist' and 'post-socialist' European countries in their perceptions and interpretations of 'the traditional Irish pub session', which derive to a certain extent from cultural information historically available on a wider scale in these countries. Nevertheless each context was bound up with very culture-specific meanings that local musicians created from the cross-cultural encounters of traditional Irish music within their specific contexts.

However, one common strand that emerged from all conversations, interviews, and mini questionnaires with local musicians at these different locations was that despite influences from the mass media, radio, television, Internet, CDs, and print publications about Irish music, it was still the influence of specific Irish musicians encountered in community music-making events that informants cited as the most influential aspect for them to have become interested in playing this musical genre themselves. Also common to all European session contexts investigated in this chapter was that hierarchies were established in relation to length of involvement with this genre, but that all continental sessions were open to newcomers. This is likely to have come about because no images of 'Celtic fringe authenticity' were ascribed to these community music-making activities by their related state institutions.

Obviously an instrumental musical genre will mean different things to different people, but it is quite evident from these case studies that so many community musicians at different European locations are really dedicated to playing this genre. Meeting regularly to learn and exchange new items of repertoire requires a fair amount of commitment, and we can also observe that they invest quite a bit of work into improving their playing styles with cultural sensitivity, in agreement with the musicological genre rules and following examples from their musical role models. The sometimes voiced fear within Irish home contexts that taking the Irish pub session to different countries will 'muddy the pure drop of the music' seems not very convincing because – as this ethnographic study shows – musicians in other countries do not just 'pick up nice Irish melodies'. Cultural associations travel abroad with the music, where they are creatively adapted by local musicians to their local contexts, and in the process new meanings emerge. It is exactly these flexible adaptations that support, and give meaning to, 'the tradition', because traditions can only exist if they are flexible enough to adapt to the requirements of their environment. Cultural conditions within the Irish home context have also changed over time, and traditions that are not adaptable to changing circumstances are soon forgotten (cf. Hobsbawm and Ranger 1983). So it is indeed the cross-cultural encounter of the Irish pub session that strengthens and contributes to continually recreating the tradition of this musical genre.

CHAPTER 6

The Elusive Celt

In this chapter we will take a closer look at the images of the 'elusive Celt' – as they have made their appearance in relation to 'Celtic music' – and where they may come from. To do this it stands to reason to start with an overview of what we know about the historical Celts, for instance through conjectures from archaeological finds and ancient Greek and Roman text references to Celtic tribes.

We will then proceed to investigate what images have been associated with the ancient Celts and Celtic culture, in the past and at present. By paying attention to linguistic evidence for the interconnection of Celtic languages we will consider consequences of conflating people with languages and present-day associations between Celtic languages and 'authentic local culture'. We will investigate why the image of the elusive Celt remains so powerful in present-day art, music, writing, and other cultural productions, as well as in related identity constructions. We will question who may benefit from upholding images of the elusive Celt by reflecting on the ethnographic descriptions in Chapter 5, and why the construction of ethnic nationalism keeps reappearing in the music of areas that have been termed 'the Celtic fringe'. We will close this chapter by suggesting how community practices of traditional Irish music session playing can contribute to gradually adapting the images of the 'elusive Celt' to a less divided future in Europe by letting go of old images that were built on antagonistic oppositions of 'self' and 'other'.

Dissecting Celtic Seed Dispersals

Let us start this discussion of the 'elusive Celt' with a brief overview of what regions archaeological research has linked with Celtic cultural centres and Celtic migrations. The oldest evidence of Celtic settlements seems to relate to the south of present Germany at around 1000 BC, from which the *Hallstatt* and the *La Tène* cultures appear to have emerged in the seventh to fifth centuries BC[1] The centre of the *Hallstatt* culture is said to have been located in present Austria and parts of southern Germany, whereas the *La Tène* culture had its centres in present France and partly in present Bohemia/Czech Republic. After this time, if one leaves aside discussions of transhumance necessities and political conquests, the Celts appear to have been 'happy wanderers' to various regions: north, south, east, and west. John Haywood (2001) locates them in present Spain before 500 BC, in present Italy between 390 and 300 BC, in present Greece around 280 BC, in the immediately following years in central Anatolia (Galatia), and between 320 and 200 BC migrating eastwards in the region north of the Black Sea. In the second century BC the Romans seem to have driven the in Europe remaining Celts northwards, where Celtic culture then arrived in England, Wales, Scotland, and Ireland.

Simon James (1999:57) raises the interesting question of whether it may have been material objects and fashions that may have moved around in Europe, rather than people named 'Celts', but in any case cultural fashions now associated with the elusive Celt did spread far and wide in the late Bronze Age, as evidenced by archaeological finds. The *Fischer Lexikon* (Vol. 5:3178) mentions that most European names of rivers are derived from the culture of the Celts. Matthias Schulz (1997) cites archaeology confirming that in prehistoric times Celtic tribes resided all over present Europe, that Turin, Budapest, and Paris were founded by the Celts, and that a Celtic tribe – the Parisii – gave their name to Paris. This leaves us with a

---

1   Historian/Early Celts specialist, Nora Kershaw Chadwick, locates *Hallstatt* culture in the Early Iron Age, at c 800–450 BC, and *La Tène* culture in the Late Iron Age, in the period from c 450 BC. According to her assessment, many archaeologists identify the emergence of the Celts with the close of the Bronze Age, through the *Hallstatt* period and down to *La Tène* (Dillon and Chadwick 1967:1–2).

situation where most regions in Europe, and quite a few regions beyond, could lay claim to Celtic ancestry in their culture, but most certainly not all of them do. Therefore the question remains what 'Celtic' means within different cultural contexts.

Malcolm Chapman (1992) and Desi Wilkinson (1999) – among others – refer to the contemporary category of 'Celtic countries' as comprising Ireland, Scotland, Wales, Cornwall, Brittany, and Galicia, and according to Fernandez (2000) there exists also an emic claim to inclusion in this category in neighbouring Asturias. So we can say that at the present point in time these countries/regions have established internationally recognised links to be 'Celtic cousins'. But what about the other regions where Celts have left their cultural footprint, such as for instance the areas imprinted by the *La Tène* and *Hallstatt* cultures? Patrick O'Neill (1982:43) reminds us that the Celts' 'first homeland as a distinguishable people was the valleys of southern Germany, Austria and Bohemia', although Chapman (1992:39) and Wilkinson (1999:238) add that some people – such as the ancient Greeks – did not regard 'Celtic' and 'Germanic' people as different cultural groups. It can be taken for granted that this will have led to confusions in later readings of historical texts.

Leaving aside for the moment the question whether cultural artefacts can be equated with the spread of ancient people, it would seem that based on the theory of ethnic Celts in Europe, all countries where my research was carried out could have laid claim to 'Celtic roots'. As it happens, most of them didn't do so, but Turkey is rather different in this regard. Barry Cunliffe (2003:71) voices the opinion that the migrating Celts who crossed into central Anatolia in the third century BC, may have retained the name 'Galatians', but did soon abandon all traces of *La Tène* culture, to mix with the culture of the region in which they found themselves. As it turns out, present-day Irish and Turkish musicians in Istanbul have in recent years been cooperating in composing and performing music together that they describe on their CD covers as 'Celtic traditional tunes which are performed in an eastern way, the inspiration [for which] comes from the Galatians'. No doubt there are a lot of commonalities between Irish and Turkish traditional musical genres. For instance, traditional Irish music is centred on micro-variations of melodies, using infinite fine ornamentation, and

sometimes drone accompaniment. All these traits it shares with much of
Turkish traditional music. There are indeed such a lot of commonalities that
in his 1960s series of radio programmes (published as Ó Riada 1982) the
famous Irish composer and musician, Seán Ó Riada, described traditional
Irish music as being closer to Middle Eastern than to European music:

> Irish music is not merely not European, it is quite remote from it. It is, indeed, closer
> to some forms of Oriental music. The first thing we must do, if we are to understand
> it, is to forget about European music. Its standards are not Irish standards; its style
> is not Irish style; its forms are not Irish forms. (Ó Riada 1982:20)

Obviously Ó Riada is referring by 'European music' to music from
the Western classical tradition, not to any of the numerous European
folk music genres. And his term 'oriental' sounds a little dated since
Edward Said started major academic discussions in the 1970s/80s about
Eurocentric constructions of a romantic 'other' through 'Orientalism'. But
since the elusive Celt has become the romantic 'other' to central Europe
in the late twentieth century, Ó Riada's musical comparison is maybe
matching in more than one sense. Matthias Schulz (1997) has referred
to recent archaeological findings of 'oriental looking jewellery and dress'
found in Celtic burial sites, and he quotes prehistorian, Otto-Herman
Frey, describing them as 'clearly showing Persian influences'. Evidently,
nothing will have prevented pre-historical people from exchanging orna-
mental fashions.

The question of whether commonalities between Irish and Middle
Eastern musical genres have been transmitted among 'Celtic cousins' since
the third century BC, or whether they are cultural image constructions of
recent centuries, is of course a completely different question – which it
is impossible, however, to decide either way. The conditions seem a little
reminiscent of the old question of whether the bodhrán has a centuries-old
history as a drum in Ireland or not. In his 1960s series of radio programmes
about Irish music, Seán Ó Riada (1982:75–6) voiced the opinion that 'the
bodhrán dates back probably to the Bronze age, and possibly earlier'. Some
writers like to believe that digging up evidence for such conjectures might
be possible (cf. Lange 2004), but I would tend to think that if archaeologists
were to dig up the remains of a centuries-old bodhrán, the skin of drum

heads and wooden frames would have completely disintegrated, and the only remains they might find would be bits of rusty nails.

I doubt whether anyone would venture to propose a theory that such bits of rusty nails can be counted as evidence for the existence of bodhráns in previous centuries. Likewise, however, it is impossible to prove that bodhráns did *not* exist for centuries, as the only dug-up evidence possible could be bits of rusty nails. So my point is that any historical evidence of migrating musical styles over centuries/millennia would be at least as elusive as buried rusty nails. Or as Albert Einstein is famously quoted as having said once: 'The answer is yes or no, depending on the interpretation.'

Either way, it should not be necessary to answer this question, as our interest within this present frame of inquiry focuses on how evidence of 'the roots of the elusive Celt' is constructed, interpreted, and negotiated in late twentieth-/early twenty-first-century Europe. Fintan Vallely's *Companion to Irish Traditional Music* (1999) defines 'Celtic music' as a 'fanciful term which expresses a world-view or record-shelf category rather than actual links between musical genres'. This seems quite a minimalist definition, as it disregards all the many and varied identity and image constructions in various parts of the world that do or do not claim Celtic links for their musical genres.

Let us instead take a look at the contemporary (Canadian – Irish/Scottish) recording artist, Loreena McKennitt, who has worked extensively with Middle Eastern, Irish, and other musicians, and who provides some interesting clues about this topic on her promotional CD (1991), issued with the special-edition CD *The Visit*. On the cover of this CD set she provides an interpretation of 'the elusive Celt' that may well accompany us through to the end of this chapter:

> From our vantage point, thousands of years later, the Celtic imagination seems boundless, knowing no parameters to mark the real and the surreal. Their art conveys the spiritual and supernatural powers so evident in many of their legends and myths. They have bridged many ages, mixing East and West, and provided a fascinating legacy that lives on today as strong as ever. (McKennitt 1991)

Here we have the perfect construction of the 'romantic other', based on myth and legend (with its origins in the nineteenth century), and encompassing 'timeless times' and 'boundless regions': the perfect ingredients for conveying an image of 'the elusive Celt'.

The accompanying CD contains an interview of Loreena McKennitt (by Tim Wilson), where she provides a little more detail of her ideas about 'the Celtic' and possible links with Middle Eastern music. Bearing in mind that she has extensively and most successfully worked together with Turkish and other musicians, and that her sometimes ethereal sounding arrangements very skilfully combine western and eastern musical styles, it can be said that her interpretation and image construction of 'the Celtic' has led to positive and highly interesting results. In her 1991 interview with Tim Wilson she describes her personal musical development thus:

> I was very intrigued by very early eastern influences of the Celts, of the Celtic people … Many people, when they hear of 'Celts', think of the Irish, Scottish, Welsh, English … They [the Celts] are believed to have come from eastern Europe, and perhaps from as far back as India and north Africa. (McKennitt 1991)

Here we have a fine example of twentieth-century Celtic-myth-in-the-making: eastern Europe, India, Africa – the Celts as the eternal romantic 'other'. Intuiting the intended meanings, Tim Wilson then interprets 'Celtic' as a cradle-of-culture concept for indigenous world musics with many different flavours. This concept agrees nicely with Malcolm Chapman's (1992, 1994) analysis of present-day 'Celtic music' as a fixed-label category with highly flexible contents.

To get a better grasp of 'the elusive Celt', Tim Wilson then asks Loreena McKennitt about her own 'Celtic roots', to which she describes 'working with her father with livestock, which grounded her Celtic'. I was just beginning to imagine a brown and a white bull on their farm,[2] when charmingly she blows her own myth:

> People think I'm from the west coast of Ireland. I was familiar with the Arthurian legends. But I was introduced to Celtic music around 1977/78 in a Winnipeg folk club. (McKennitt 1991)

---

2   A reference to the legend of the Cattle Raid of Cooley.

Unfortunately she does not explain here what this 'Celtic music' was. It may have been the label, or the concept, or any of the above-mentioned musical styles; or maybe it was just an inspiration of 'the elusive Celt':

> My music is difficult to define. I don't wince at the label 'New Age', but New Age music is not focused, and my music *is focused*. So in this regard it is not 'New Age'. (McKennitt 1991)

So the focus of the interview is still on applying musical labels (which are likely to turn out hollow categories with flexible contents). I should say here that I really like many of Loreena McKennitt's musical arrangements, with their delightful combinations of stylistically eastern and western roots, and more than one of her compositions could stand as a musical representation of 'the elusive Celt', but at this point it seems that she is not going to help us get any closer to the conceptual essence of this 'elusive Celt'.

On the other hand the related question arises of why there is an international need to construct such a multicultural mega-category. Is the present-day Celt just a replacement of the former 'Oriental'? Have cultural labels changed with twenty-first-century political developments? Does the 'elusive Celt' stand for multicultural transcendence? To answer these questions I shall return to the possible interpretations that some of my academic colleagues have offered.

Certainly groundbreaking work as regards the construction of such images in society has been carried out by Gabriele Haefs in her published PhD thesis 'Das Irenbild der Deutschen' (Haefs 1983), which presents a study of images of Irish folk musicians in 1970s Germany. Many of her observations are too period-specific to be considered here, but she provides such interesting descriptions as German and Scandinavian audiences of this period often considering the bodhrán to be particularly 'traditional' because the 'term sounds traditional to them' (Haefs 1983:114–5).

This is a most relevant point that gets easily overlooked in academic studies, as some images obviously just emerge by coincidence of fanciful terminology. And to pre-empt a possible argument: they are not and cannot be planned. For instance, the Irish word *feadóg* for the equally popular tin whistle in Irish traditional music did never evoke any such image constructions at all. So we should keep in mind that at least some emerging images are rather coincidental.

Somewhat different is the case as regards images of Ireland as the home of 'saints and scholars' and the *insula magica* where everything seems possible. Here we move into the realm of the 'Celtic fringes' of Europe, and in her study of images of the Irish in German literature, Doris Dohmen (1994) traces these 'otherworldly' image constructions to a long European literary tradition that reaches back into previous centuries. Even further back in time goes Patrick O'Neill's (1982) study, which tries to trace the roots of the Irish stereotype in Europe back to around the sixth century, the time of an exodus of Irish monks to the continent. O'Neill comes to the conclusion – and Dohmen agrees with him on this point – that stereotypical images have a tendency to persist, irrespective of people's [in this context: Germans'] experience of the Irish in their midst.

In *Call to the Dance* (2016) Desi Wilkinson has cast a finely observing eye on changes in the associated meanings of 'Celtic' versus 'Breton' in Brittany over the last four decades, from which a clear picture emerges how such images are in a constant process of slow fluctuation and transformation through multiple influences. However, whatever the reasons for changing associations with the term 'Celtic' in post-*Riverdance* Ireland and Europe and an imagined blossoming fraternity of 'Celtic cousins' in many different regions of the world may be, it is *Irish* music that is played in the growing number of pub sessions in countries that are presently *not* considered 'Celtic cousins'. But then, musical categories seem to be among the most malleable in the world. Keeping in mind the recent inclusion of Australia as a participant in the Eurovision Song Contest (2015), it would seem wise for the Japanese Irish session musicians in Japan described by Sean Williams (2006) to refuse being integrated into the worldwide maelstrom of 'Celtic cousins' if they wish to preserve their 'essential Japanese aesthetic principle of unrequited longing' when playing Irish music in their local pub sessions.

The positive strand of this development has been described by Martin Stokes (1994:6) as 'Celtic music' being potentially easy, participatory, and crossing national boundaries. The not so positive strand shows in the term 'Celtic' becoming increasingly meaningless. To decide whether this is cultural colonialism pussyfooting in a new guise or not, we will have to look ethnographically at who is benefiting from these mega-inclusions, and who is carrying them forward. In descriptions of the contested 'authenticity' of Irish music in the 'Celtic fringes' of County Clare (O'Shea 2008, Kaul 2009) we have seen that image creations of *Bord Fáilte* can lead to unpleasant encounters based on ethnic boundary constructions at community level music-making. For Rosemary McKechnie (1993) it led to the surprising discovery that common marginality constructions between Corsicans and Celts resulted in her being regarded as 'Celtic' in Corsica. These perceptions of Corsicans were based on images of 'fellow marginal communities' being seen in much the same way as the 'Celtic fringes'.

The idea that 'Celticity' in the 'Celtic fringes' is based on ethnicity has not just been deconstructed by argumentation (Chapman 1992, James 1999), but has also been underpinned by a recent survey on genetic structure in the 'British Isles' (Leslie et al. 2015), which comes to the conclusion that there is no evidence of a general 'Celtic' population in non-Saxon parts of the United Kingdom and that DNA investigations did not support the 'Celtic dispersal' explanation. This does not mean, however, that the concept of a 'Celtic dispersal' to the 'Celtic fringes' cannot continue to be used for cultural constructs.

Obviously in Brittany 'Celticity' – or *Celtitude*, as Desi Wilkinson prefers to call it – has grown into a fully developed 'Celtic cousin' industry, with 'Celtic' merchandise for tourists and their annual *Festival Interceltique* at Lorient, and Scotland has now its own annual *Celtic Connections Festival*, these days taking place in Glasgow, with hundreds of musicians from around thirty countries participating in this weeklong event. As Wilkinson (2016:27) has described it, 'this [Celtic fringe] is metaphorically growing taking in increasing numbers of would-be Celts from other European regions and locations much further afield like Brazil'. As we have seen, this does not apply to all European countries, most likely because they do not fit in with the existing image of the 'Celtic fringes'.

But what about the original Celtic homelands in Europe surrounding the area of the former Iron Curtain? Southern Germany certainly does not claim any 'Celticity', and neither does Austria. However, in both countries traditional Irish music is much loved, and locally organised regular community sessions of Irish music are widespread, and they are quite popular with their associated insider community. So at least here there seems to exist no connecting link between interest in Irish music and claims to 'Celticity', possibly motivated by interests to preserve the 'romantic other'.

The Czech Republic may on occasion officially admit its historical 'Celticity' – for instance in introductory speeches at Bernard's Summer School – but it is not a popular concept among the Irish music community. When I asked some community musicians about the image of Celtic connections, they rejected the possibility that their local music might be labelled as 'Celtic'. I certainly did not find any evidence of 'Celtic' merchandise on offer anywhere (except in direct connection with the *Irish Music Summer School*, which is dedicated to Irish culture and is discussed in detail in Chapter 5). There are a good few Irish bars in Prague, but their live music is frequently focused on American popular music, with the occasional set of traditional Irish tunes integrated into their programme. This means that selling 'Celticity' or 'Celtic cousin' culture to visiting tourists does not seem here an option at all.

In Chapter 5 I have described the community of dedicated players of Irish music in Prague who organise their sessions flexibly in local non-Irish bars and their motivations for this. Czech bands focusing on playing Irish music frequently choose Irish language names for their outfit (e.g. *Dún an Doras, Le hAnam, Poitín, Dálach*), and recording artistes may employ the label 'Celtic' for their category of music if this seems a viable option within specific contexts. However, they relate this to playing 'Irish music', and in session playing they do not mix it widely with any of their own folk genres. My further questioning about the possible label 'Celtic' within this cultural context elicited remarks that 'in the Czech Republic we have a mixture of cultures, including Celtic and Slavic, and it does not seem meaningful to stress one of these'. We might summarise this view as 'culturally fertile compatibility', which hints at European identity constructions rather than at 'Celtic cousin' aspirations.

The south of France, home to the ancient Celtic *La Tène* culture, certainly has no claims to becoming a 'Celtic cousin' either. There exists, however, a network of international musicians interested in meeting for traditional Irish session playing, who coordinate their meetings through the Internet (FB: Irlande TradFr). I found out about this from Dominique Renaudin whom I met playing in Irish sessions in Istanbul. As we have seen above, community Irish session playing – a culture child of the 1960s – can become quite popular in any one country without any attempts to establish connecting links as a 'Celtic cousin' culture.

Further south-east along the trail of the former Iron Curtain, in Budapest as well as in Bucharest, neither Irish session playing nor 'Celtic cousin' culture seem to be a topic of any interest at all. In Budapest, Irish music appears to be a speciality interest of a few musicians who meet privately, somewhat clandestine like in the GDR, where playing Irish music in public venues was illegal. Official claims of staff in Budapest Irish bars indicated that their musical interests were directed towards American culture. In Bucharest, tourist bar music offers were more internationally oriented, including Balkan musical genres, but even in Irish bars I found only an occasional input of Irish music, and certainly no claims to becoming a 'Celtic cousin' culture.

Rather different is the situation in Istanbul, and I was indeed surprised to find that a local Irish pub, the *James Joyce* (see Figure 5.22), has been hosting traditional Irish music sessions since 1999. Organised by locally resident Irish fiddle player, Eamonn Lehane, on a weekly basis (excepting holiday periods), the session attracts Irish, English, American, and other visiting international participants as well as Turkish musicians. And some of the latter do indeed find the term 'Celtic' meaningful for their musical choices. Some session participants are members of *Celteast*, a group of Turkish musicians who came together in 2007 with the intention of using inspiration from the pre-Christian Celtic Galatian culture of central Anatolia, to perform and create a synthesis in their music between Anatolian and Balkan melodies and traditional tunes of the presently internationally recognised 'Celtic cousins', which they define on the cover of their CD *Made in Istanbul* (see Figure 5.24) as Ireland, Scotland, Wales, Isle of Man, Cornwall, Brittany, and Galicia. For this CD they have collaborated in 2011/12 with Eamonn Lehane, and it features some of their *Celteast* compositions and arrangements as well as songs written by Eamonn Lehane. *Celteast* group member, Nilüfer Ketenci, told me that she finds these ancient Celtic connections interesting, but that they are not important for her music-making. She mentioned, however, the *Ufuk Baş Ariğ* archaeological project at Ege University (in Izmir province), a cross-border Turkish-Bulgarian research project with an interest in the Anatolian Celtic connection, whose staff members organise occasional 'Celtic Festivals' with historical re-enactments in Thrace. So we can observe that there is an active interest in Turkey to explore the Anatolian Celtic connection. Whether these cross-cultural academic interests survive the 2016 political upheavals in Turkey remains to be seen, but they were certainly in existence during my fieldwork there in 2012 to 2015.

In a certain sense we could then say that 'Celtic cousins' are still migrating in Europe, even if nowadays more in spirit than in person. However, the community of musicians in Istanbul were little concerned with academic theories of Celtic history, because of their understandable focus on practical music-making. They may employ the label 'Celtic' if it facilitates selling their musical products within specific categories on the international market, or if it offers favourable conditions for cross-cultural explorations in their music-making. But either way these community musicians in Istanbul see Irish music as well compatible with Turkish (and Balkan) folk music. Suna Simsek, another Irish session musician in Istanbul, told me in response to my question about 'Celtic connections': 'I find in Irish music something really close to my culture, but I would not know what to call it.'

Might it be the Turkish wandering *aşık* musician/poet of the eternal Celtic spirit? To diffuse any possible objections to the drawing of this mythical connection, it is well to remember that the present-day 'Celtic' is to an overwhelming extent the creation of present-day human imagination. If many people feel touched by a 'Celtic spirit of music and poetry', then this influence certainly exists, and through people's perception it becomes a force for further imagination and creation.

This connection was forcefully brought home to me in relation to Italy, which I had originally not included in my itinerary for investigations into possible claims to Celtic connections because my research travel through Europe had been drawn towards Istanbul, and from conversations with Italian musicians in Belfast I had not expected any constructions of 'Celticity' in Italy. But then Paul O'Connor, a fellow music researcher whom I met in 2012 in Istanbul, drew my attention to the Italian group

Whisky Trail, who have been involved with Irish/Celtic music since the 1970s. My subsequent research into their back catalogue led to a discovery of 'the Celtic spirit in full flight'. Over time, *Whisky Trail* have arranged and combined traditional Irish/Scottish/Breton/Galician material with their own compositions in matching style, adding harmonising voices and integrating art music techniques to the mix. Not surprisingly, they have collaborated with musicians from different parts of the world, including a fair number of well-known Irish musicians.

Most interesting in this present context is that in the process of working on their seventh album, *The White Goddess* (1997), *Whisky Trail* discovered a 'Celtic cousin' connection: Robert Graves's proposition that the mythical Irish goddess *Danu* of the *Tuatha de Danaan*, is really the pre-Achaean Mediterranean *Danaë*, great mother of life, brought by them to Ireland when they were expelled from Greece in the second millennium BC (Graves 1961:64). Thus *Whisky Trail* have found a connection of ancient Irish culture to Mediterranean origins, which they interpret as the goddess *Danaë* having given to the patriarchal Celts their love of nature as a female source of inspiration for their music and poetry. Subsequently, *Whisky Trail* have recorded further concept albums, for instance *The Great Raid* (2002), themed on the *Táin* and the Cattle Raid of Cooley.

For other albums, such as *Celtic Fragments* (2013), *Whisky Trail* have combined classical (medieval) Irish poetry with contemporary influences of W. B. Yeats and their own compositions and arrangements. Their music could maybe be said to be equally traditional and innovative, and if one is given to fanciful language, one could describe it as 'the Celtic spirit again in full flight'. And as this spirit keeps wandering in the mythical realm of music and poetry, we find ourselves back in the 'timeless times' and 'boundless regions' of the 'elusive Celt'.

Anthropologists – among others – have observed that real time and virtual time are not necessarily the same, and also that the Celtic perception of time was circular. It should come as no surprise then that by focusing on myth, music, and poetry, the musicians wander effortlessly through centuries and millennia. However, there is another observation emerging from this example, namely how indeed many different countries could easily become 'Celtic cousins' if they had a strong and focused interest in establishing such connections. Sadly I missed the 1991 exhibition *I Celti* in Italy that Simon James (1999:19) mentions, from the theme of which it appears that a certain interest exists to establish 'Celtic cousin' images; at least on an institutional level such as in Romania.[3]

Certainly there are Italian musicians with a strong dedication to Irish music. For instance, Antonio Breschi (1970s founder member of *Whisky Trail*) – who has also jokingly referred to himself as 'Anthóni O'Breskey' – has extensively collaborated with other Italian and Irish musicians. But Antonio Breschi himself nowadays plays many musical genres and fusions, and in any case even a strong personal interest of musicians in Irish music does not necessarily imply any intention to highlight common historical Celtic roots, as we have seen above in cultural examples of various other European countries.

This seems to indicate that from the emic perspective of community musicians the increasing worldwide interest in the present-day interpret-ation of what is 'Celtic culture' is not a political movement, nor indeed one with underlying political aspirations. This does not mean, however, that it was not historically created from political motivations, in connection with the rise of nation-states in Europe in the nineteenth century. Certainly we can observe the present Irish session to be a clearly identifiable case of 'in-vention of tradition' (cf. Hobsbawm & Ranger 1983), because present-day cultural associations with 'the elusive Celt' have very little in common with the culture of the ancient historical Celts. Even the Irish pub session, which often serves abroad as an indicator of 'Celtic culture', has its 'ancient' roots only in the 1960s. One could of course argue that 'the world is speeding up' (cf. Sheldrake 1981, 1988), and that half a century can well establish a musical tradition. But for the cultural Celts of the twenty-first century, with their 'timeless times' and 'boundless regions' of myth and legend, such constricting historicity is of little concern.

3   *The Rough Guide to World Music* (1994:3) states that 'pockets of Celtic tradition survive in parts of Italy and Turkey', but provides no further information what and where these might be. Among musicians I heard mentioned occasional Irish sessions in Milano and Rome, but found these too casually organised to make out any specific dates.

We could possibly apply the concept of 'an imagined community' in Benedict Anderson's (1983) sense for people worldwide who share an interest in 'Celtic music', but in its presently developing form it is certainly not one with a nationalist agenda – rather one with a post-nationalist agenda, since participation is open to everyone and easily crosses national boundaries. However, neither could 'Celtic music' be described as 'anything goes'. It may be a highly flexible category with varying contents, but its performing participants have an active interest in maintaining cultural links with 'the elusive Celt'. This may seem like a tautological or circular argument, but who can confidently say that they can judge what musical or poetic inspirations guide twenty-first-century performers of 'Celtic music'? Maybe a component of it is what Gudeman & Rivera (1990) have described as 'voices in the air', only partially conscious cultural instructions from the past that are being carried over from previous times into present-day conceptualisations. But then again, a focus on such an interpretation may do injustice to people who are actively and creatively constructing present-day images of 'Celtic culture'.

Scott Reiss (2003), who has tried to unwrap and disentangle the 'Celtic phenomenon' that has grown and developed since the 1990s, sees it as essentially created and expanded by the world music recording industry (Reiss 2003:158–61), with an interest to keep the boundaries of 'Celtic music' extremely vague, so as to be able to conflate styles to make many musics fit into one bin in the record stores. A similar point has been made by Goffredo Plastino (2003) about the label 'Mediterranean music', which is also a category with highly flexible contents. This is certainly a valid point that has exerted major influences on the development of 'Celtic music' since the 1990s.

Corporate interests in the construction of 'Celtic' musical categories have also been the focus of Shannon Thornton's study in Los Angeles music shops. It describes how *Tower Records'* world music CD section uses categories according to country (in alphabetical order), for which the country with the highest volume of product serves as the main category for a number of sub-categories. In this way, 'Celtic', 'British', and 'Scottish' appear here as sub-categories of 'Ireland' (Thornton 2000:24). In this way musical categories can be constructed as neither informed by culture (musical styles, language), nor by elective affinity (ideological/spiritual concepts, New Age associations). In other words, the categories are constructed arbitrarily as desired, according to context.

Reiss's other argument, however, that 'Celtic music' is not shared, but exchanged as cultural product, and that it only exists within a virtual community of audio and video technology, is less convincing. I would think that it depends on the degree to which people – musicians and audiences – of a country embrace the label of being a 'Celtic country'. If people meet at 'Interceltic festivals', renew, revive, and create musical traditions, and play, sing, and dance together, then this is not a virtual community. Indeed, Reiss (2003:165) recognises this double aspect of 'Celtic music' in his concluding remark: 'Notwithstanding its media-driven nature, Celtic music has always had at its heart traditional musicians making the music they learned in their musical communities.'

So it seems that again it is impossible to define the distinguishing marks of what is 'Celtic music'. Traditional Irish music, which Reiss describes as strongly connected to locality and musical community (2003:163), also makes use of audio and video technology. Moreover, Irish traditional music is frequently seen as one of the most essential components in the category of 'Celtic music'. And although some traditional Irish musicians vehemently would reject the label 'Celtic' for their musical activities, others happily just make use of the labels that they find in existence. Reiss relates the following anecdote to illustrate his point:

> Martin Hayes, a recording artist and fiddler from Co. Clare currently living in Seattle, has a travel story that illustrates this eloquently: 'If somebody sees my fiddle case on an airplane, say, and asks me what I play I say "Celtic music". If I were to say Irish music he likely wouldn't know what I was talking about' (personal communication). (Reiss 2003:146)

So again it is context that determines what label is used to refer to any particular music. Like in M. C. Escher's graphic art works with multiple perspectives, it is possible to see particular musical phenomena from quite different viewpoints that can be equally valid. So the differentiation between 'community-based' and 'media-driven' may provide a useful concept to think about these different – and also partly overlapping – musical categories, but at the bottom line it will not enable us to capture the 'elusive Celt' either.

Indeed we cannot even determine for certain how 'Celtic' present-day 'Celtic music' is. Was the genre invented in the twentieth century? Or did it emerge over previous centuries, gaining its label as 'Celtic music' in the process? Gearóid Ó hAllmhuráin (1998:14) states confidently that 'Modern Celtic music … has no historical basis whatever in the music of the ancient Celts'. However, almost in the same breath he confirms that '… these Iron Age warriors have left few traces of their own music, songs or dances'. James (1999:29) thinks that characteristic cultural traits such as language, rich oral traditions, music, and material arts were ascribed to the Celts as part of a conception of a typical Celtic society. We may have no evidence of the actual music of the ancient Celts, but to me non-evidence of existence does not constitute evidence of non-existence. That there is absolutely no connection between music of the ancient Celts and modern 'Celtic music' may be likely, but it is no more than an assumption. Who can say with total conviction that it was not a flapping butterfly wing in the tenth century BC in present Bohemia or southern France (*Hallstatt* & *La Tène*) that carried musical 'voices in the air' to present-day locations where people perceive and reconstruct them into 'Celtic music'?

Such a process could also be explained by Rupert Sheldrake's (1981) concept of *morphic resonance*. According to his theory, cultural inheritance works over time and space through morphic fields, and it does not depend on direct contact between person and person for the transmission of cultural traits. Such morphic fields do not weaken over time, they gain strength with every repetition of their specific cultural traits anywhere in the world. For this process the cultural traits need not be *exactly* the same; they can rather work like a composite photograph that results from many very similar traits (cf. Sheldrake 1981:123–4).

Sheldrake (1988:289–91) suggests this concept as an explanation for examples of parallel evolution, which anthropologists had unsuccessfully tried to explain through diffusionism, a theory that faltered when they considered parallel cultural traits that appeared independently in continents that had never had any contact with each other. Sheldrake originally developed his theory of *morphic resonance* in relation to the natural world, but later extended it to social and cultural aspects of human societies, in particular as an influence on the development of cultural traditions (Sheldrake 1988:263–5).

It is certainly a most useful concept for explaining the phenomenal worldwide spread of the Irish pub session in the twentieth century, which can definitely not be explained solely by direct inter-human contact. But even adding the influence of the media and the Internet does not provide a sufficient explanation. Just because something appears on the Internet does not necessarily mean that it will become popular, and the media will soon lose interest if any musical genre shows no audience attention. But the most interesting aspect is that it is not just the musical genre that has travelled worldwide, but concepts about the performance context and extra-musical behaviour, sometimes termed 'session etiquette'. A theory of morphic fields that store such social memory in connection with musical memory offers a possible explanation for the sudden worldwide spread of the Irish pub session. And as Sheldrake points out, *morphic resonance* is not a *sole* explanation for phenomena, it is complementary to other processes such as those mentioned above.

If we use Sheldrake's theory to explain the powerful emergence of 'Celtic music' in the twentieth century, it would lead us to infer that the present 'Celtic seed' must have fallen upon a fertile cultural field from the past. Which it may well have done, since Sheldrake (1988:188–9) points out that phenomena of atavism can also be expected in the social and cultural realm. However, this approach does not lead to any conclusive evidence either, and so the 'elusive Celt' has slipped out again from under our fingers.

Grace Clunie and Tess Maginess (2015:19) offer a more spiritually themed explanation that 'the Celtic' as a concept of 'the Celtic Spirit' is recycled through art forms to match the requirements of different historical periods. For their theory it would therefore not be necessary for a congruence to be present between different artistic manifestations over time, as the glue that holds it all together is of a spiritual nature that can find different expressions. I would not argue with their concept, but it brings us in no way any closer to capturing the 'elusive Celt'. Indeed the 'Celtic Spirit' seems even a little more elusive for an analysis than the Celts themselves.

On the other hand it cannot be denied that by discussing the topic we are contributing to the contemporary construction and reconstruction of 'the Celtic'. This means we are in no different position than all these musicians worldwide who play 'Celtic' or 'definitely not Celtic' music. And like all these musicians, we have no influence over others interpreting our position as favouring one or another interpretation. But then, a musical study – of whatever genre – is under no obligation to offer definitive answers. Presenting the mosaic of cultural interpretations at different locations presents a flexible option for views that readers must in any case develop for themselves. It is also the only possible option since cultural interpretations and constructions of 'the Celtic' are always negotiable – invoked, confirmed or negated within specific cultural contexts – and therefore given to change at any time, at whatever location, no matter what their historical roots may be.

It is exactly these flexible characteristics of the Celtic image that have enabled this more or less hollow category (Chapman 1992) to become so powerful by being filled with diverse imaginations and creations. Or, as Moya Kneafsey (2002:137) has argues, it is this 'elusive, ill-defined nature of the Celts' that keeps them interesting and also open to exploitation by commercial interests. To which I would add that it is not just commercial interests that profit from the elusive image of the Celts but creative inspirations, some of them of a spiritual nature, and not least of all for activities of community music-making. To get a clearer idea of how such processes of community appropriation of Celtic imagery come into being, let us have a look at the example of 1970s Brittany.

Constructing Celticity: The Example of 1970s Brittany

Desi Wilkinson (1999, 2016) has described Alan Stivell as having played a pivotal role in establishing a perceived connection between musics of the countries that are presently regarded as Celtic in the 1960s/70s in Brittany. It seems that Stivell succeeded in doing this by drawing on the historical commonality of the Bardic harp in these different regions, and

Figure 6.1. Cover of Alan Stivell's album *Renaissance of the Celtic Harp*

then using its image to draw together repertoires from different historical periods and Celtic regions to establish a common Celtic identity.

According to Stivell's back catalogue, his first recording, *Telenn Geltiek/ Harpe Celtique*, dates from 1964, although international recognition is more closely linked with the album *Renaissance of the Celtic Harp* (1971) (see Figure 6.1), which presents repertoires from various regions perceived as Celtic, in arrangements that address middle class tastes as well as interests of folk community musicians. As is well known now, this was a very successful move, as the instrument was particularly well suited to sell the concept of 'the Celtic' to a broad audience.

In support of its concept, the cover of the *Renaissance of the Celtic Harp* presents an image of a harp ornamented with spiralling Celtic carvings as its sole focus. Over twenty musicians who have participated in this recording are only mentioned by name in relation to the instruments they played. These instruments range from Breton bombarde, Irish flute, and

Scottish bagpipes to tablas, organ, electric guitar, viola, cello, and double bass. So it seems that Stivell's music could have been equally well used to sell 'world music fusion' as for 'Celtic music', and the overlap of the present concept of 'Celtic music' with 'world music' is likely to have at least some roots in Stivell's influential move to sell 'Celtic music' in this arrangement.

Undoubtedly the highlighting of Celtic roots in Brittany in the 1970s was influenced by the successes of the folk revival in Ireland at this time. On the folk side of stressing this Celtic connection we find ballad groups like *Tri Yann*, who have also been active since this time, but who were also influenced by what was going on at this time in the European folk revival movement. Many folk revival musicians of the 1970s integrated songs from other regions or countries into their repertoire if they fit into the concept of their musical stage presentations. Some people may argue that *Tri Yann* were to some extent sitting on a fence because they are from Nantes, a non-Breton speaking part of Brittany, which is by some people even contested as being part of Brittany at all. But of course people's identity constructions need not agree with contemporary political boundaries at all.

In this regard *Tri Yann's* 1972 album makes a clear statement: *Tri Yann an Naoned* (see Figure 6.2) is Breton for 'the three Jeans from Nantes'. The musicians – Jean-Paul, Jean-Louis, Jean, and Bernard – regard themselves as from Brittany, and they identify with the cultural concept of 'Celtic countries'. The album contains Breton, Irish, Scottish, and Québecois material; the Breton material is partly in the Breton and partly in the Gallo/French language. To these musicians 'Celticity' resides not so much in musical qualities, but in the timeless quality of Celtic mythological themes, and the 'boundless regions' aspect of 'the Celtic' serves to unify linguistically different parts of Brittany.

Tri Yann's arrangements include a variety of folk instruments – as was a common occurrence of many groups in the 1970s folk revival – such as jews harp, harmonica, banjo, glockenspiel, and the Irish bodhrán, and this also applies to their 1973 album *Dix Ans – Dix Filles*, which again features Breton material in Breton as well as in French.

Their 1974 album *Suite Gallaise* (see Figure 6.3) brings this aspect even more to the fore. The repertoire selection includes French language songs, an Irish language song, and a traditional Breton set of dance music

Figure 6.2. Cover of *Tri Yann*'s album *An Naoned*

from the *Bretagne Gallaise* region. The sleeve notes highlight the opinion that Breton language songs are not the sole repository of Breton song culture. In particular, the song *Complainte de la blanche biche* is described as an example of dealing with Celtic themes in the French language. This is an aspect that is also touched upon by Desi Wilkinson (2016:120), who mentions that *complaintes* (lamentations) in French or Gallo (which is linguistically close to French) are also sometimes sung in the traditional call and response style, and that song collectors in *Basse Bretagne*, whose interest was closely focused on Breton language material, may have neglected to pay attention to such songs in the repertoire of their informants.

The French versus Breton language aspect is a major bone of contention in the musical repertoire of Brittany. In *Call to the Dance* (2016) Wilkinson describes in detail how local Breton community musicians and cultural activists in the 1970s looked to the Irish example of traditional music festivals and *fleadhanna*, leading them to develop the *fest-noz* (and

Figure 6.3. Cover of *Tri Yann*'s album *Suite Gallaise*

fest-deiz) community dance events, which in turn led to a major revital-isation of Breton musical culture. According to Wilkinson (2016:16) the annual *Festival Interceltique* in Lorient includes even fringe events of Irish session playing in local pubs as an informal attraction for visitors to par-ticipate in 'Celtitude'.

However, after the 'Elusive Celt' had successfully taken flight in Brittany, the movement seems to have developed its own momentum, and according to Wilkinson's observations over the last four decades, local 'Celtitude' identity constructions have been transformed to lean increas-ingly towards 'Bretonnitude' identity constructions in Brittany. The latter seems to be closely aligned with Breton language aspects and traditional dance music repertoires associated mostly with Breton speaking regions. This is an interesting aspect, because what emerges clearly from Wilkinson's four decades of study in Brittany is that, although a number of musical in-struments from the Irish tradition were adopted into this specialised group of musicians playing for traditional Breton dance community events, the dissimilarity of the respective musical styles was never questioned during the 1970s heydays of developing Celtic cousin culture perceptions.

Undeniably there are thematic as well as musical similarities that one can observe and stress, or deny, between many musical genres, depending on cultural policies and interests of the day and place. In his concluding observations of the Breton traditional music scene in the early twenty-first century Wilkinson (2016:143) notes that the 'Celtitude' period of the 1970s looks increasingly like it may have been a phase, and that, while some musicians now feel confident to construct their identities around a sense of 'Bretonnitude', others turn their attention towards fusions with other genres such as Balkan and Middle Eastern musics. This is a fine confirmation that musical cousin genres and associated identities are open to changing interpretations, influenced by their time and place.

For me, the most interesting aspect that emerges from Wilkinson's study is that this whole process of cultural revival was in the first instance initiated by musicians themselves, and that in the long run it had a most positive outcome for Breton traditional music and dance culture. Of course, Alan Stivell and *Tri Yann* were not the only musicians involved in the 1970s construction of a Celtic cousin culture in Brittany; they just stand here as examples to show how the whole process was brought forward by Breton musicians of this period.

So in conclusion we can observe that at this time in Brittany the 'Elusive Celt' was perceived to reside as much in lyrical qualities of poetry as in the symbolism of particular musical instruments, rather than in the stylistic qualities of the actual music. That the recording industry would take the meaning of the contents of the label 'Celtic music' into a rather different and ever widening direction was not foreseeable at this time, and could just as well have led somewhere completely different.

Conclusion

In this chapter we have taken a cursory look at the development of the image of the 'elusive Celt' from Bronze Age warrior to romantic inspirer for music and poetry in our present-day society. We have then taken a detailed look at how 'Celticity' is constructed and applied nowadays and how an ideological application of conflating people and languages has led to the creation of what are at present considered to be 'Celtic countries'. By recourse to scientific research we have refuted the argument that present 'Celticity' may be based on ethnicity and on dispersal of the ancient Celts to Europe's 'Celtic fringes'. All evidence from fieldwork and other research indicates clearly that 'Celticity' is a cultural construct and that playing present-day 'Celtic music' has nothing whatsoever to do with ethnicity. It is a concept that can be appropriated by different groups in society for different purposes, which may indeed be happening at present in relation to community music-making of traditional Irish music in an increasing number of countries.

Conclusion

In this study we have looked closely at the changing images of traditional Irish music by paying attention to ethnographic detail at six European locations and at the many guises of the ever 'elusive Celt' in contemporary European culture. Research locations were selected for the purpose of comparing influences of recent history on the related image constructions on both sides of the former Iron Curtain in Europe. We have investigated the multiple roles of 'the Celt' as a member of an ancient ethnic group; as identifier for linguistically related geographical regions; as inspiration for imaginative spiritual and artistic creativity; as a label for musical categories; as a basis for constructs of imagined ethnicity, individual identities, and political boundary constructions; as claimed proof for different aspects of authenticity; and as a conceptual forerunner of the present European Union. In the process we have discovered that the 'elusive Celt' is a very powerful cultural construct that for its effectiveness depends essentially on its flexibility.

Genetic survey investigations have proven that the theory of a Celtic dispersal to the currently termed 'Celtic fringes' is unfounded, but we discovered that this does not prevent the cultural concept from being equally applicable to any self-identified 'marginal regions', as the Corsican example has shown. Indeed O'Malley & Patten (2014:13) argue that peripherality is constructed in relation to 'the Balkans' just like to the 'Celtic fringe'. It follows from this that 'marginal regions' can be imaginatively constructed in opposition to *anywhere*.

The concept of 'community' has not proved useful for our analysis because the discussed musicians do not 'construct community' in that they do not claim general 'Celticity'. They are individual community groups, albeit with a partial overlap of participants and with common musical interests. As O'Shea (2008:134) has pointed out, the concept of a 'constructed community' idealises the processes of making music together in sessions, while in reality neither societies nor even groups of musicians are uniform. Additionally, one and the same musician may identify his/her music as 'Celtic' within one context, but not so in another. It is the very flexibility of the image of the 'elusive Celt' that makes it so powerful because its interpretations are always negotiable, depending on specific contexts and intentions. As far as can be generalised, image constructions about 'the Celtic' and traditional Irish session playing seemed to have moved further in their transitional period of connecting with western culture traits in the post-socialist contexts of the GDR and the Czech Republic than in Hungary and Romania. Especially in Prague there was evidence that community musicians actively contested remains of inflexible state ideologies from their socialist past, so as to accommodate socio-musical contexts associated with contemporary Irish session playing. This had, however, nothing whatever to do with attempts to establish links with geographic 'homeland' regions of the ancient Celts. Indeed, the only re-gions where such connections were emphasised were in Turkey, but only on a community basis for integrating 'eastern Celtic' and 'western Celtic' musical genres, and for a joint academic project between universities in Anatolia and in the Balkan region.

No matter what ideological interpretations may tell us, at the bottom of it, *all* ethnicities are social constructs because we are all humans, but we are all individually different. This point has very succinctly been brought out by Bill Rolston (1999:45) in relation to contemporary political song in Northern Ireland by summarising that all ideologies create myths, all ideology is a form of 'invention of tradition', and that all history operates on the basis of selecting from the past, but that there are nevertheless es-sential differences in how people from what they see as 'self' or 'other' groups in society create social meanings through their music. It does not matter whether we construct the cultural 'other' because we want to feel superior or because we ascribe to him elusive qualities that we ourselves desire. Tes Slominski (2020:18) has argued that 'hierarchies are built into both national and humanist systems, in which some people are human and others are not quite human … Irish trad is the inheritor of these systems'. This conclusion leads her to plead for abandoning ethnic nationalism as a framework for understanding vernacular music traditions. The present study has confirmed that ethnicity is indeed a very unreliable measure for grounding category constructions.

As far as the traditional Irish session is concerned, it is very interesting to observe that it remains a vernacular tradition when travelling to diverse European community contexts of aficionados of this genre. At all investigated contexts community musicians asserted that their main influence and primary inspiration for playing this genre were locally resident Irish musicians. This proves that despite wide availability of written and online resources the face-to-face contact remains the essential primary means for passing on this musical genre. It can be inferred that this constitutes an essential determining factor for its popularity that has contributed to the international spread of the Irish community session. The use of the image of the 'elusive Celt' remained flexible and negotiable within all these community contexts, making its appearance noticeable mostly in the context of selling locally made CDs of 'Celtic music'. In this way the 'elusive Celt' is preserved but remains forever elusive.

Let us remember that the image of the 'elusive Celt' is a very powerful one in contemporary society. It may be imaginary, but it persists and we cannot make it disappear by identifying it as illusory. We can, however, contribute to its transformation because images are constructed by people and are therefore always open to negotiation, re-interpretation, and change of their meaning. As the *I Celti* exhibition of 1991 in Venice has grounded its thematical message, all Europe shares in the inheritance of having descended from ancient Celtic tribes that migrated around Europe, and this can serve as a unifier just as well as constructing a cultural 'other'. Murray G. H. Pittock (1999:141) has argued that 'one of the major features of Celticism today is its internationalism and Europeanism', and Kaul (2009:7) echoes this sentiment by describing the traditional Irish music experienced within his research contexts in Doolin, County Clare, as having 'become a vehicle for cosmopolitanism'. I would think the genre has certainly potential to free us from time-worn squabbles over labels such as 'my music', 'your music', or 'our music'. It is a positive influence that the 'elusive Celt' can contribute to Irish traditional music. Maybe this is indeed the image in the direction of which the 'elusive Celt' is going. We all have a choice how we use the image; let us use Irish traditional community music creatively and let us contribute to make the 'elusive Celt' a unifying rather than a divisive influence in the future.

References

Bibliography

Anderson, Benedict, 1983, *Imagined Communities: Reflections on the Origin and Spread of Nationalism*, London: Verso.

Baily, John, 1977, "Movements in Playing the Herati Dutar", pp. 275–330 in *The Anthropology of the Body*, ed.: J. Blacking, London: Academic Press.

Barta, Peter I. (ed.), 2013, *The Fall of the Iron Curtain and the Culture of Europe*, New York: Routledge.

Beckerman, Michael, 1996, "Kundera's Musical *Joke* and 'Folk' Music in Czechoslovakia, 1948-?", pp. 37–53 in *Retuning Culture*, ed.: M. Slobin.

Berger, Peter, and Thomas Luckmann, 1967, *The Social Construction of Reality,* Harmondsworth: Penguin.

Blacking, John (ed.), 1977, *The Anthropology of the Body,* London: Academic Press.

Blaustein, Richard, 1993, "Rethinking Folk Revivalism: Grass-Roots Preservationism and Folk Romanticism", pp. 258–74 in *Transforming Tradition,* ed.: N. V. Rosenberg, Champaign: University of Illinois Press.

Bogyay, Katalin, 2013, "Foreword" in *The Fall of the Iron Curtain and the Culture of Europe*, ed.: Barta, New York: Routledge.

Bohlman, Philip V., 1988, *The Study of Folk Music in the Modern World*, Bloomington and Indianapolis: Indiana University Press.

Borneman, John, 1992, *Belonging in the Two Berlins,* Cambridge: Cambridge University Press.

Boullier, Dianna, 1998, *Exploring Irish Music and Dance*, Dublin: O'Brien.

Bowers, Jane, and Judith Tick (eds), 1986, *Women Making Music: The Western Art Tradition 1150–1950,* London: Macmillan.

Brace, Geoffrey, 1968, *The Story of Music,* Loughborough: Wills & Hepworth.

Breathnach, Breandan, 1971 (1977), *Folk Music and Dances of Ireland*, Cork: Mercier.

Brennan, Helen, 1999, *The Story of Irish Dance,* Dingle: Brandon.

Buchanan, Donna A. (ed.), 2007, *Balkan Popular Culture and the Ottoman Ecumene: Music, Image, and Regional Political Discourse*, Lanham, MD: Scarecrow Press.

Buek, Fritz, 1926, *Die Gitarre und ihre Meister,* Berlin: Schlesingersche Buch- und Musikhandlung Lienau.

Burke, Peter, 1992, "We, the People: Popular Culture and Popular Identity in Modern Europe", pp. 293–308 in *Modernity and Identity*, eds: S. Lash and J. Friedman, Oxford: Blackwell.

Carson, Ciarán, 1986, *Pocket Guide to Irish Traditional Music,* Belfast: Appletree.

Chapman, Malcolm, 1992, *The Celts: The Construction of a Myth*, New York: St Martin's Press.

Chapman, Malcolm, 1994, "Thoughts on Celtic Music", pp. 29–44 in *Ethnicity, Identity and Music: The Musical Construction of Place,* ed.: M. Stokes, Oxford: Berg.

Cheyne, Sandy, 1994, *Die Irische Kneipenszene in Berlin,* self-published.

Clunie, Grace, and Tess Maginess, 2015, *The Celtic Spirit and Literature*, Dublin: Columba Press.

Cohen, Anthony P. (ed.), 2000, *Signifying Identities: Anthropological Perspectives on Boundaries and Contested Values*, London and New York: Routledge.

Cohen, Sara, 1994, "Identity, Place, and the 'Liverpool Sound'", pp. 117–34 in *Ethnicity, Identity and Music,* ed.: M. Stokes, Oxford: Berg.

Cunliffe, Barry, 2003, *The Celts: A Very Short Introduction*, New York: Oxford University Press.

Danaher, Kevin, 1959, "Hunting the Wren", pp. 667–72, *Biatas*, XIII (9), December.

Dillon, Myles and Nora Kershaw Chadwick, 1967, *The Celtic Realms*, London: Weidenfeld and Nicolson.

Dohmen, Doris, 1994, *Das deutsche Irlandbild: Imagologische Untersuchungen zur Darstellung Irlands und der Iren in der deutschsprachigen Literatur*, Amsterdam: Rodopi.

Dowling, Martin, 2014, *Traditional Music and Irish Society: Historical Perspectives*, Farnham: Ashgate Publishing Ltd.

Epstein, Dena J., 1975, "The Folk Banjo: A Documentary History", pp. 347–71, *Ethnomusicology*, 19 (3).

Feintuch, Burt, 1993, "Musical Revival as Musical Transformation", pp. 183–93 in *Transforming Tradition,* ed.: N. V. Rosenberg, Champaign: University of Illinois Press.

Fernandez, James W., 2000, "Periperal Wisdom", pp. 117–44 in *Signifying Identities,* ed.: A. P. Cohen, London and New York: Routledge.

Finnegan, Ruth, 1989, *The Hidden Musicians: Music-Making in an English Town*, Cambridge: Cambridge University Press.

Frigyesi, Judit, 1996, "The Aesthetic of the Hungarian Revival Movement", pp. 54–75 in *Retuning Culture*, ed.: M. Slobin.

Frith, Simon, 1983, *Sound Effects: Youth, Leisure and the Politics of Rock 'n' Roll*, London: Constable.

Frith, Simon, 1996, *Performing Rites: Evaluating Popular Music,* Oxford: Oxford University Press.

Gilroy, Paul, 1993, *The Black Atlantic: Modernity and Double Consciousness*, London: Verso.

Görner, Rüdiger, 2013, "Borders in the Mind or How to Re-invent Identities", pp. 48–57 in *The Fall of the Iron Curtain and the Culture of Europe*, ed.: Barta, New York: Routledge.

Graves, Robert, 1961, *The White Goddess: A Historical Grammar of Poetic Myth,* London and Boston: Faber and Faber.

Gudeman, Stephen, and Alberto Rivera, 1990, *Conversations in Colombia: The domestic Economy in Life and Text*, Cambridge: Cambridge University Press.

Haefs, Gabriele, 1983, *Das Irenbild der Deutschen,* Frankfurt am Main: Land Verlag.

Hale, Amy and Philip Payton (eds), 2000, *New Directions in Celtic Studies,* Exeter: University of Exeter Press.

Hamilton, Colin (Hammy), 1977, *The Session: A Socio-Musical Phenomenon*, MA Thesis, Queen's University Belfast.

Hannan, Robbie, 1996, "Pipers Call the Tune", pp. 48–9, *Causeway Journal*, IV (Winter).

Harker, Dave, 1985, *Fakesong: The Manufacture of British Folksong 1700 to the Present Day*, Milton Keynes: Open University Press.

Harrington, John P. and Elizabeth J. Mitchell, 1999, *Politics and Performance in Contemporary Northern Ireland*, American Conference for Irish Studies, Amherst: University of Massachusetts Press.

Harvey, David C., Rhys Jones, Neil McInroy and Christine Milligan (eds), 2002, *Celtic Geographies: Old Cultures, New Times*, London: Routledge.

Haywood, John, 2001, *The Historical Atlas of the Celtic World,* London: Thames & Hudson.

Henebry, Richard, 1928, *A Handbook of Irish Music*, Dublin and Cork: Cork University Press.

Hobsbawm, Eric and Terence Ranger (eds), 1983, *The Invention of Tradition,* Cambridge: Cambridge University Press.

James, Simon, 1999, *The Atlantic Celts: Ancient People or Modern Invention?*, London: British Museum Press.

Joshi, Baburao, 1963, *Understanding Indian Music,* Bombay: Asia Publishing House.

Kaul, Adam R., 2009, *Turning the Tune: Traditional Music, Tourism, and Social Change in an Irish Village*, New York and Oxford: Berghahn.

Kirchenwitz, Lutz, 1993, *Folk, Chanson und Liedermacher in der DDR: Chronisten, Kritiker, Kaisergeburtstagssänger*, Berlin: Dietz Verlag.

Kneafsey, Moya, 2002, "Tourism images and the construction of Celticity in Ireland and Brittany", pp. 123–38 in *Celtic Geographies: Old Cultures, New Times*, eds: D. Harvey et al., London: Routledge.

Lange, Moritz Wulf, 2004, *Handbuch für Bodhránspieler*, Hamburg: Schell Music.

Langlois, Tony, 1996, "The Local and Global in North African Popular Music", pp. 259–73 *Popular Music*, 15(3).

Leslie, Stephen, Bruce Winney and Garrett Hellenthal, 2015, "The Fine-scale Genetic Structure of the British Population", pp. 309–19, *Nature*, 519, 19 March.

Levin, Theodore, 1996, "Dmitri Pokrovsky and the Russian Folk Music Revival Movement", pp. 14–36 in *Retuning Culture,* ed.: M. Slobin, Durham: Duke University Press.

Ling, Jan, 1997, *A History of European Folk Music*, Rochester: University of Rochester Press (Translation from Swedish, 1998, Akademiförlaget).

MacDonagh, Oliver, W. F. Mandle and Pauric Travers (eds), 1983, *Irish Culture and Nationalism, 1750–1950,* Dublin: Gill and Macmillan.

Macdonald, Sharon (ed.), 1993, *Inside European Identities*, Oxford: Berg.

Malcolm, E., 1983, "Popular Recreation in 19th Century Ireland", pp. 40–55 in *Irish Culture and Nationalism,* eds: O. MacDonagh et al., Dublin: Gill and Macmillan.

McCarthy, Pete, 2000, *McCarthy's Bar*, London: Hodder and Stoughton.

McCrickard, Janet E., 1987, *The Bodhrán: The Background to the Traditional Irish Drum*, Glastonbury: Fieldfare Arts.

McKechnie, Rosemary, 1993, "Becoming 'Celtic' in Corsica", pp. 118–45 in *Inside European Identities*, ed.: S. Macdonald, Oxford: Berg.

McNamee, Peter (ed.), 1992, "General Discussion", pp. 48–54 in *Traditional Music: Whose Music?*, Queen's University Belfast: Institute of Irish Studies.

Mitsui, Toru, 1993, "The Reception of the Music of American Southern Whites in Japan", pp. 275–93 in *Transforming Tradition*, ed.: N. V. Rosenberg, Champaign: University of Illinois Press.

Moloney, Mick, 1992, Irish Music in America: Continuity and Change, PhD Thesis, Villanova University of Pennsylvania.

Moloney, Mick, 1999, "Acculturation, Assimilation and Revitalisation: Irish Music in Urban America", 1960–1996, pp. 125–34 in *Crosbhealach an Cheoil – The Crossroads Conference 1996*, eds: F. Vallely et al., Dublin: Whinstone.

Murphy, Pat, 1995, *Toss the Feathers: Irish Set Dancing*, Dublin: Mercier.

O'Donnell, Marie Louise and Jonathan Henderson, 2017, "'One step above the greenery': A Survivor's Guide to Playing to an Audience Who Does Not Listen", pp. 50–65 in *Musicians and Their Audiences*, eds: I. Tsioulakis and E. Hytönen-Ng, London: Routledge.

O'Flynn, John, 2009, *The Irishness of Irish Music*, London and New York: Routledge.

Ó hAllmhuráin, Gearóid, 1998, *Pocket History of Irish Traditional Music*, Dublin: O'Brien Press.

O'Keefe, Máire, 1999, "Tradition versus Change: The Irish Button Accordion", pp. 160–5 in *Crosbhealach an Cheoil*, eds: F. Vallely et al., Dublin: Whinstone.

O'Malley, Aidan and Eve Patten (eds), 2014, *Ireland West to East: Irish Cultural Connections with Central and Eastern Europe*, Oxford: Peter Lang.

O'Neill, Francis, 1903, *O'Neill's Music of Ireland*, New York: D. M. Collins.

O'Neill, Francis, 1907, *The Dance Music of Ireland,* Chicago: Lyon & Healy.

O'Neill, Francis, 1913 (1973), *Irish Minstrels and Musicians,* East Ardsley, Yorkshire: EP Publications.

O'Neill, Patrick, 1982, "Ireland and Germany: A Survey of Literary and Cultural Relations before 1700", Part I and II, pp. 43–54 and 152–65, *STUDIES: An Irish Quarterly Review, 71.*

Ó Riada, Seán, 1982, *Our Musical Heritage,* Portlaoise: Fundúireacht an Riadaigh/ Dolmen Press.

O'Shea, Helen, 2008, *The Making of Irish Traditional Music*, Cork: Cork University Press.

Pittock, Murray G. H., 1999, *Celtic Identity and the British Image*, Manchester and New York: Manchester University Press.

Plastino, Goffredo (ed.), 2003, *Mediterranean Mosaic*, New York: Routledge.

Rasmussen, Ljerka Vidić, 1996, "The Southern Wind of Change: Style and the Politics of Identity in Prewar Yugoslavia", pp. 99–116 in *Retuning Culture,* ed.: M. Slobin, Duke University Press.

Reiss, Scott, 2003, "Tradition and Imaginary: Irish Traditional Music and the Celtic Phenomenon", pp. 145–69 in *Celtic Modern,* eds: M. Stokes and P. Bohlman.

Rolston, Bill, 1999, "Music and Politics in Ireland: the Case of Loyalism", pp. 29–56 in *Politics and Performance in Contemporary Northern Ireland*, eds: J. P. Harrington and E. J. Mitchell, University of Massachusetts Press.

Rosenberg, Neil V. (ed.), 1993, *Transforming Tradition: Folk Music Revivals Examined*, Urbana and Chicago: University of Illinois Press.

Sacks, Oliver, 1985, *The Man Who Mistook his Wife for a Hat*, London: Picador.

Sacks, Oliver, 1995, *An Anthropologist on Mars,* London: Picador.

Said, Edward W., 1978, *Orientalism,* London: Penguin Books.

Santos, Caetano Maschio, 2020, "(Hy-) Brazil, Celtic Land? An Ethnomusicological Study of the Formation and Characteristics of the Irish-Celtic Music Scene in Brazil", pp. 41–60, *Ethnomusicology Ireland*, (6).

Schiller, Rina, 1994, Traditional Irish Music: A Study of Musical Instruments and Gender Aspects, BA Dissertation, Queen's University Belfast.

Schiller, Rina, 2001, *The Lambeg and the Bodhrán: Drums of Ireland,* Belfast: QUB Institute of Irish Studies.

Schiller, Rina, 2004, Traditional Irish Music in Berlin: Musical Exchange in a European context, PhD Thesis, Queen's University of Belfast.

Schiller, Rina, 2010, "Monstertunes for Sally's Garden: Transforming Images of Place Through Musical Performance", pp. 19–22, *Irish Journal of Anthropology*, 13(1).

Schulz, Matthias, 1997, "Fahndung im Druidenland: Archäologie", pp. 134–42, *Der Spiegel* (31).

Scully, Judy, 1997, "A 'stage Irish Identity' – An Example of 'symbolic power'", pp. 385–98, *New Community*, 23(3).

Seeger, Charles, 1977, *Studies in Musicology 1935–1975*, Berkeley and London: University of California Press.

Sheldrake, Rupert, 1981 (2009), *A New Science of Life*, London: Blond & Briggs.

Sheldrake, Rupert, 1988, *The Presence of the Past: Morphic Resonance and the Habits of Nature*, London: Harper Collins.

Silverman, Carol, 2007, "Trafficking in the Exotic with 'Gypsy' Music: Balkan, Roma, Cosmopolitanism, and 'World Music' Festivals", pp. 335–61 in *Balkan Popular Culture and the Ottoman Ecumene*, ed.: D. A. Buchanan, Lanham, MD: Scarecrow.

Slobin, Mark, 1993, *Subcultural Sounds: Micromusics of the West*, New England: Wesleyan University Press.

Slobin, Mark (ed.), 1996, *Retuning Culture: Musical Changes in Central and Eastern Europe*, Durham and London: Duke University Press.

Slominski, Tes, 2020, *Trad Nation: Gender, Sexuality, and Race in Irish Traditional Music*, Middletown: Wesleyan University Press.

Smith, Graeme, 1997, "Modern-Style Irish Accordion Playing: History, Biography and Class", pp. 433–63, *Ethnomusicology*, 41(3).

Smith, Graeme, 2003, "Celtic Australia: Bush Bands, Irish Music, Folk Music, and the New Nationalism", pp. 73–91 in *Celtic Modern*, ed.: M. Stokes, Lanham: Scarecrow.

Smith, Michael, 1999, *Never Again! More Fascinating Facts about Ireland*, Belfast: White Row Press.

Stokes, Martin, 1992, *The Arabesk Debate: Music and Musicians in Modern Turkey*, Oxford: Clarendon Press.

Stokes, Martin (ed.), 1994a, *Ethnicity, Identity and Music: The Musical Construction of Place*, Oxford: Berg.

Stokes, Martin, 1994b, "Introduction: Ethnicity, Identity and Music", pp. 1–27 in *Ethnicity, Identity and Music*, Oxford: Berg.

Stokes, Martin, 1994c, "Place, Exchange and Meaning: Black Sea Musicians in the West of Ireland", pp. 97–115 in *Ethnicity, Identity and Music*, Oxford: Berg.

Stokes, Martin and Philip V. Bohlman (eds), 2003, *Celtic Modern*, Lanham, Maryland and Oxford: Scarecrow Press.

Stokes, Martin, 2004, "Music and the Global Order", *Annual Review of Social Anthropology*, 33, 47–72.

Stokes, Martin, 2010, *The Republic of Love: Cultural Intimacy in Turkish Popular Music*, London and Chicago: University of Chicago Press.

Svašek, Maruška, 2006, *Postsocialism: Politics and Emotions in Central and Eastern Europe*, New York: Berghahn Books.

Tansey, Seamus, 1996, "Irish Traditional Music: the melody of Ireland's soul; it's [sic] evolution from the environment, land and people", pp. 211–3 in *Crosbhealach an Cheoil – The Crossroads Conference 1996*, Dublin: Whinstone.

Taylor, Timothy D., 1997, *Global Pop: World Music, World Markets,* New York and London: Routledge.

Thornton, Shannon, 2000, "Reading the Record Bins: The Commercial Construction of Celtic Music", pp. 17–29 in *New Directions in Celtic Studies,* ed.: A. Hale, Exeter: Exeter University Press.

Tsioulakis, Ioannis, 2011a, "'At first I saw it as a toy': Life Stories, Social Consciousness and Music Ethnography", pp. 19–28, *Irish Journal of Anthropology*, 14(1).

Tsioulakis, Ioannis, 2011b, "Jazz in Athens: Frustrated Cosmopolitans in a Music Subculture", pp. 175–99, *Ethnomusicology Forum*, 20(2).

Tsioulakis, Ioannis and Elina Hytönen-Ng (eds), 2017, *Musicians and Their Audiences: Performance, Speech and Mediation*, London: Routledge.

Tsioulakis, Ioannis, 2021, *Musicians in Crisis: Working and Playing in the Greek Popular Music Industry*, London: Routledge.

Turino, Thomas, 2008, *Music as Social Life: The Politics of Participation,* Chicago and London: University of California Press.

Uí Ógáin, Ríonach, 1996, "From Camden Town to Ros an Mhíl – Changes in the Connemara Singing Tradition", pp. 226–33 (219–26) in *Crosbhealach an Cheoil – The Crossroads Conference 1996,* F. Vallely et al. (eds), Dublin: Whinstone.

Vallely, Fintan, 1998, "Gucci Paddy: Fintan Vallely Points the Purist Finger", pp. 37–41, *Graph*, 3.2.

Vallely, Fintan (ed.), 1999, *The Companion to Irish Traditional Music,* Cork: Cork University Press.

Vallely, Fintan, Hammy Hamilton, Eithne Vallely and Liz Doherty (eds), 1999, *Crosbhealach an Cheoil – The Crossroads Conference 1996,* Dublin: Whinstone Music.

Vallely, Fintan, 2003, "The Apollos of Shamrockery: Traditional Music in the Modern Age", pp. 201–7 in *Celtic Modern*, ed,: M. Stokes, Lanham: Scarecrow.

van de Port, Mattijs, 1998, *Gypsies, Wars and other Instances of the Wild: Civilization and its Discontents in a Serbian Town*, Amsterdam: Amsterdam University Press.

Walker, Brian M., 2019, *Irish History Matters: Politics, Identities and Commemoration,* Brimscombe Port: History Press Ireland.

Watson, Lyall, 1973, *Supernature,* London: Hodder and Stoughton.

Wilkinson, Desi, 1991, "Play me a lonesome reel", MA Dissertation, Queen's University Belfast.

Wilkinson, Desi, 1999, The World of Traditional Dance Music in Brittany, PhD Thesis, University of Limerick/Ollscoil Luimnigh.

Wilkinson, Desi, 2002, "Euro-Paddy Land: The Irish cultural diaspora in Europe", pp. 9–11, *Journal of Music in Ireland,* 2(5).

Wilkinson, Desi, 2003, "'Celtitude', Professionalism, and the *Fest Noz* in Traditional Music in Brittany", pp. 219–56 in *Celtic Modern,* ed.: M. Stokes and P.V. Bohlman, Lanham: Scarecrow.

Wilkinson, Desi, 2011, "From Donegal to Senegal: An Experience of the Process of Collaboration in Intercultural Ensemble Practice", *ICTM* online journal.

Wilkinson, Desi, 2016, *Call to the Dance: An Experience of the Socio-Cultural World of Traditional Breton Music and Dance,* Hillsdale, NY: Pendragon Press.

Williams, Sean, 2006, "Irish Music and the Experience of Nostalgia in Japan", pp. 101–19, *Asian Music,* 37(1).

Williams, Sean, 2010, *Focus: Irish Traditional Music,* New York: Routledge.

Williams, William H. A., 1996, *'Twas Only an Irishman's Dream': The Image of Ireland and the Irish in American Popular Song Lyrics, 1800–1920,* Urbana and Chicago: University of Illinois Press.

Reference Works

Fischer Lexikon, 1979, Frankfurt/Main: Fischer.

The New Grove Dictionary of Music and Musicians, 1980, London: Macmillan.

The New Grove Dictionary of Musical Instruments, 1984, London: Macmillan.

Rough Guide to World Music, 1994, London: Penguin (eds: Simon Broughton, Mark Ellingham, David Muddyman and Richard Trillo).

Videography

Crossing the Bridge: The Sound of Istanbul, 2005, documentary film by Fatih Akin, narrator: Alexander Hacke, 90 mins, Bavaria Film International.

Der Fiddler von Dooney: Irland zwischen den Zeiten, 2001, NDR, März Film, 90 mins, written and directed by Peter Leippe.

Edward Said: The Last Interview, 2005, documentary film by Mike Dibb, recorded in 2002, interviewer: Charles Glass, 208 mins, Drakes Avenue Pictures Ltd.

Discography

Bottlewash Band, 2006, *Straight From the Bottle,* self-published.

Bradfield, Dave, 1995, *Celtic Pulse,* self-published.

Dún an Doras, 1999, *Bossa Nudski,* Mars Records (no number).

Dún an Doras, 2003, *Sweet & Sour,* Indies Records MAM 222-2.

Dún an Doras, 2005, *Rua,* Indies Records MAM 266-2.

Irish Weavers, 2001, *The Work of the Weavers,* self-published.

Lehane, Eamonn & Celteast, 2012, *Made in Istanbul,* Şölen Kaset Müzik P.11.34.Ü.341.

McKennitt, Loreena, 1991, *'The Visit'* (collector's edition), Quinlan Road/Warner Bros. 9 26880-2 (with promotional CD: PRO-CD 5554).

Poitín, 2014, *Wish,* self-published.

Poitín, 2016, *Simple Pleasures*, self-published.

Shanahan, John and Marty Byrne, 2003, *Paddy on the Spree,* self-published.

Smyth, Eddie and Marty Byrne, 2000, *The Toetapper,* self-published.

Spinning Wheel, 2011, *The Maid on the Shore,* SPIN-02.

Stivell, Alan, 1971, *Renaissance of the Celtic Harp,* Philips 6414 406.

Tri Yann, 1972, *Tri Yann an Naoned,* Marzelle, Phonogram 510 771-2.

Tri Yann, 1973, *Dix Ans – Dix Filles,* Marzelle, Phonogram 510 773-2.

Tri Yann, 1974, *"Suite Gallaise"*, Marzelle, Phonogram 510 772-2.

Whisky Trail, 2013, *Celtic Fragments,* Materiali Sonori 99106.

Index

Printed by
CPI books GmbH, Leck